HIDDEN HISTORY *of*
★ TENNESSEE ★
POLITICS

HIDDEN HISTORY *of*
★ TENNESSEE ★
POLITICS

JAMES B. JONES JR.

THE
History
PRESS

Published by The History Press
Charleston, SC 29403
www.historypress.net

Unless otherwise noted, images are courtesy of Tennessee State Library and Archives (TSLA).

First published 2015

ISBN 9781540212856

Library of Congress Control Number: 2015938493

Notice: The information in this book is true and complete to the best of our knowledge. It is offered without guarantee on the part of the author or The History Press. The author and The History Press disclaim all liability in connection with the use of this book.

Dedicated to my wife, Cynthia, and my son, Boyd.

CONTENTS

PREFACE

This book is intended to provide the reader with information concerning unique episodes and personalities in Tennessee's history. The narratives of filibustering, politics, political figures, struggle against monopoly and unique editorial art are part of the entire mix of the past, generally unknown or hidden from view not because they are unimportant but because the focus of history has been on the famous personalities and great events in our past. The stories presented here are, for the most part, a blend of lesser incidents and personalities that are generally unknown, concealed from our knowledge of Tennessee's past. The chapters that follow fill in part of a blank space, allowing the reader to better understand the Volunteer State's past as something other than a series of names, events and, worse, dates. One might think of these articles as speed bumps that oblige us to slow down and look at our surroundings, allowing us to scan other things that may have been unseen as we hurry by. The accounts in this book are neither fictitious nor folklore but real events in Tennessee's past. They have been carefully researched, using archival sources, letter collections, diaries and journals, as well as secondary sources, to provide authenticity to their content. I am optimistic you will find them interesting and even educational. The phrase "the rest is history" is appropriate here. What happens in the past between the great events and dates? Quite a lot, as it turns out. In this book I try to make it clear that some events do not have the grandeur of celebrated events or personalities but have a dignity of their own, one common theme being that they have been obscured by almost singular attention to big events in "the progressive line" of history. Tennessee's history is full of such lesser-known episodes, and to ignore them is to overlook and discount that part of the past that is essential to knowing where we come from and where we are going, to use a customary phrase. The chapters in this book are part of "the rest" of history that are now no longer hidden but open, no longer in the "the dustbin of history."

1
THE LOST STATE OF FRANKLIN

TENNESSEE'S FIRST INSTANCE OF SECESSION

In American history, the period from 1783 to 1789 was characterized by turmoil. The Revolution had been ended by the Treaty of Paris in 1783, and the United States government was provided for by the Articles of Confederation. Under the articles, the states held the power, and under the Constitution the central government was supreme over the states. The turbulence caused by the change was a backdrop to the fascinating and complex story of the rise and fall of the Lost State of Franklin. The story of the State of Franklin is a bewildering drama with ramifications at the frontier, state, national and even international levels. It is also a demonstration of how Tennessee's pioneer founders sought a solution to problems presented in the relentless movement to the west.

Those who pioneered in East Tennessee in 1772 formed their own government, a representative democracy. This government, named the Watauga Association, had the first written constitution among white pioneers west of the Appalachian Mountains. They were carrying on an already established tradition of self-government established in the original thirteen colonies. The association was in place when the American Revolution began in 1775.

The land these pioneers settled belonged to the State of North Carolina. In the late spring of 1784, one year after the end of the American Revolution, the North Carolina legislature transferred all of its western land (principally what is today Tennessee) to the American government under the Articles of Confederation. This act of cession on the part of North Carolina would help to stimulate many people in what are today Washington, Sullivan and Greene Counties to meet and create a government of their own. Since the land no longer belonged to North Carolina, it only seemed right and proper to some to establish their own state in the west. It was necessary also because the old arrangement with the state had resulted in an inequitable situation for the trans-mountain settlers. Indeed, many North Carolinians believed the over-mountain folk were no more than "offscourings of the earth" or "fugitives from justice." This did not endear the settlers to North Carolina. In December of that year, representatives met and decided they were ready to form a state, free from the control of its former parent. The way was clear. The new jurisdiction was to be called the State of Franklin and was formed on August 23, 1784, when delegates of the Watauga Association met in Jonesborough. The three counties of Washington, Sullivan and Greene were declared to be independent. Another meeting would convene in a few months to draw up a provisional constitution and plan of government.

A minority led by John Tipton disagreed and wanted to remain under the rule of North Carolina. The vote was twenty-eight to fifteen, or about 65 percent in favor of independence. The next day, ballots were cast in two conflicting and competing elections. One was to select a representative to the North Carolina legislature and the other a plebiscite on the creation of the State of Franklin. The Franklinite candidates won both elections. When the North Carolina assembly met, only the Tiptonite delegates were seated. In nearly three months' time, however, on November 20, 1787, North Carolina repealed its former act of cession to the American Confederation, but the news was slow to arrive in Franklin.

This made the government of what would be called the State of Franklin illegal and its leaders open to charges of treason. The stage was set for confusion and conflict that pitted the power and intelligence of some of the state's earliest leaders against one another to decide the question.

On December 14, 1784, leaders of the Watauga settlements met to declare the independent State of Franklin's existence. A temporary constitution was adopted and the name Franklin chosen to honor Benjamin Franklin. Their declaration of independence from North Carolina ended with the attestation that "it is our own duty and inalienable right to form ourselves into a new and independent state." They did not yet know that the legislature of North Carolina had rescinded its cession made six months earlier.

By March 2, 1785, the legislative body of the State of Franklin had made a formal reply to Governor Alexander Martin of North Carolina. The petition detailed the reasons for the formation of the state out of North Carolina's

Portrait of John Sevier.

western territory. At this meeting was the governor's representative, Major Samuel Henderson, sent to the State of Franklin to ascertain what it was these people wanted. Henderson carried with him a letter, addressed to John Sevier, only recently elected governor of Franklin, inquiring what it was the Franklinites desired. Henderson learned the Franklinites wanted security for themselves, liberty and prosperity. Their fortunes would be best served by autonomy from North Carolina.

The Franklinites then carried on as though they were indeed independent. For example, during this initial assembly of Franklin, Sevier was authorized to negotiate with the Cherokee Indians. In three months, the governor of the State of Franklin concluded a treaty with the Cherokees (Treaty of Dumplin Creek) on June 10, 1785, and even attempted to expand the new state's

John Sevier as an Indian fighter.

boundaries. The Franklinites moved quickly into the territory out of which Blount County would be established in 1796.

Soon the peace was shattered, and Indian warfare resumed when whites continued to occupy territory identified as Indian land by the Treaty of Hopeful, negotiated in November 1785. Led by Sevier, the Franklinites soon triumphed over the Cherokees. In August 1786, they were forced to sign the Treaty of Coyote, permitting white settlement farther south to the Little Tennessee River. Shortly thereafter, however, the Indians attacked whites along the river, inevitably leading to white retaliation and the destruction of Indian towns all along the Hiwassee River. Sevier's forces even murdered Cherokee leaders, including Old Tassel, who had come to negotiate under a flag of truce. Sevier for a while entertained an alliance with Georgia to remove the Cherokees from the Muscle Shoals area, but the idea never came to fruition.

The State of Franklin even carried out its own fledgling foreign policy. Prior to the warfare with the Cherokees, Franklin's leaders counseled with neighboring Spanish officials. At that time, Spain controlled the territory along the Gulf of Mexico and west of the Mississippi River. Spain, because it could and felt obliged to protect its holdings, closed the Mississippi River to navigation. Moreover, Spain was making friends with western Indian tribes and encouraged secession movements among American settlements in the West. Franklinites were among those who, by 1786, were disappointed with the American national government under the Articles of Confederation. The Franklinites especially disliked Congress's policy regarding southern Indians, which they held was much too deferential. Such were the stimuli that led the Franklinites to seriously begin negotiating with Spain. Indeed, during the negotiations, Sevier was quoted by Franklinite negotiators as wishing "to place themselves under the King of [Spain]."

The Franklinites were by no means the only group in the Trans-Appalachian West who were alarmed over the possibility of forfeiting their economic lifeline, the Mississippi River. They also debated the wisdom of remaining in the American union versus joining forces with the Spanish. For example, Don Diego de Gardoqui, the Spanish diplomatic delegate, had been in communication with U.S. congressman James White of North Carolina, who had extensive landholdings on the Cumberland River.

White assured the Spaniard that western leaders would gladly secede from the United States and ally themselves with either Spain or England. Should Spain immediately open the Mississippi, then the western settlements would align with Spain, according to White. He continued his Spanish intrigue and in 1788 carried a letter from Gardoqui to Sevier denying that Spain had ever incited Indian uprisings and expressing the belief that Spain was "much disposed" to give the residents of the State of Franklin complete protection from Indian attacks.

Greatly encouraged by Gardoqui, Sevier expressed the idea that he was drawn to opening direct talks with Spain. According to Sevier, the citizens of Franklin had "come to realize truly upon what world and upon which nation depend their future happiness and security."

Franklin needed to have safe navigation on the Mississippi River and Spanish protection while Franklin's land speculators extended the boundaries of the state to the Muscle Shoals area on the Tennessee River and, last but not least, a loan of a few thousand pounds that would be repaid by the export of Franklin products to the many Spanish ports in Central and South America. In return, Franklin would cut ties with both North Carolina and the United States and swear allegiance to Spain, as long as the state could maintain control of its domestic affairs. Sevier was positive that other western pioneer communities would follow Franklin's example.

Indeed, pioneers in the Cumberland settlements also had begun talks with Spanish representatives. By 1788, they had sustained so many Indian attacks that they were willing to look to sources other than North Carolina and the United States for protection. Negotiations continued until 1789, and it appeared that both Franklin and the Cumberland settlements would ally with Spain.

Spanish suspicion of the Franklinites, however, outweighed their interest in them. One Spaniard wrote of his firm belief that the western pioneers were more willing to declare their independence from the United States than in declaring a partnership with Spain. Finally, on April 20, 1879, Esteban Miro, Spanish governor of Louisiana, sent a "Memorandum of Concessions of Westerners" that expressed the Spanish proposition. Because, wrote Miro, the United States and Spain were at peace, he could not encourage Franklin and its sister settlements to agree to annexation. If the westerners obtained their independence on their own, Spain would grant them favors "compatible with the interests of the Crown." It would be better for the Franklinites to migrate to western Louisiana, where they would be given real estate and religious freedom if they took an oath of allegiance to Spain, as twenty-two-year-old Andrew Jackson did on July 15, 1789. Becoming a subject of the Spanish crown was never more than a last recourse for the Franklinites and Cumberland settlements. By late 1789, the U.S. Constitution was ratified, and the land known as Tennessee was ceded to the central government by

North Carolina. There was no more need to parley with the Spanish, and talks ended.

In the meantime, Governor Martin was replaced by his good friend Richard Caswell as the new governor of North Carolina in the spring of 1785. Hopes seemed to be buoyed, especially after it was learned that North Carolina was being conciliatory and offering to allow Franklinites to send delegates to the North Carolina Assembly, as well as amnesty and pardons for those who had participated in the State of Franklin's formation.

This last offer by Governor Caswell split the ranks of the Franklinites into two factions: those who wished to reunite with North Carolina and those determined to see the new state remain free and independent. In support of the new state were John Sevier and his followers. Sevier maintained that he would serve his four-year term as governor of the State of Franklin. Those who wished to return to the North Carolina fold were led by John Tipton. The two would soon be antagonists in the first conflict about government in Tennessee history.

John Tipton was soon elected as the representative for the three counties to the North Carolina Assembly and, ominously, given the rank of colonel in the North Carolina militia. In this capacity, Tipton was bound to enforce the laws of North Carolina in the illegitimate State of Franklin. The stage was set for the "Battle for the Lost State of Franklin."

In Greeneville, on the last day of March 1785, the legislative body of the State of Franklin met, becoming the first legislative body ever in what would become part of the territory of Tennessee. It remained deaf to Governor Caswell's demands in April that it return to North Carolina.

Meanwhile, Governor Sevier's representative to the American Confederation meeting in Philadelphia presented the case for Franklin's joining the union. The answer, however, was negative. By August 1785, what was intended to be a permanent constitution for the State of Franklin was agreed upon, and by November 14, 1785, the legislative body of the State of Franklin had ended its first session.

For just over the next three years there were threats, counter threats, accusations, justifications and proclamations by both sides in the dispute, but nothing had been determined. David Crockett was one illustrious Tennessean born in the State of Franklin, in Limestone, on August 17, 1786. The State of Franklin acted as an independent commonwealth during this entire time. But by early 1788, the question would finally be settled.

On February 22, 1788, the open warfare between John Sevier, the governor of the State of Franklin, and his bitter political opponent, John Tipton,

Tipton-Haynes House, near the final battlefield of Sevier against Tipton in support of the State of Franklin.

began. Tipton was the elected senator for Washington County in the North Carolina Assembly and so the representative of the state opposed to Sevier. On this day, John Sevier marched to within sight of Tipton's House (now a state-owned historic site) with a party of nearly one hundred followers, "with a drum beating, Colors flying, in Military Parade and in a Hostile Manner."

Sevier sent a flag of truce and demanded that Tipton and his men surrender within half an hour and submit themselves to the laws of the State of Franklin. Tipton, who was forewarned, holed up in his house with his own force and refused to capitulate. The attack began at the end of the stipulated thirty minutes. Casualties that day included one dead horse, one wounded woman and the capture of five "Tiptonites." The battle was not yet concluded. A blockade began. Six days later, hostilities between Franklinites and Tiptonites continued as Sevier's forces carried on their siege on Tipton's farm. Rifles were fired sporadically at Tipton's home, but there were neither casualities nor any destruction to the house.

The next day, February 29, John Sevier's forces fired on a party of men coming to the assistance of Tipton. Two Tiptonites were killed, and two more were wounded. There was no victory proclaimed, and the siege of Tipton's farm continued. On March 1, John Sevier relinquished the field. His retreat took place in a blinding snowstorm. As the withdrawal took place, a Franklinite scouting party, including two of Sevier's sons, was captured by the Tiptonites. Swearing a mighty oath, Tipton threatened summarily to execute them, but cooler heads prevailed. For all practical purposes, the repression of the State of Franklin had been accomplished. But the story did not end there.

On March 2, 1788, in Washington County near Jonesborough, Senator John Tipton charged Governor John Sevier's sons with taking up arms against the State of North Carolina. They were freed on bail. Their weapons were not returned to them. Ironically, John Sevier's term as governor of Franklin expired on this date. Evan Shelby was elected to succeed him but refused to take the position. So the presidency remained vacant, and there was no leadership for what was rapidly becoming the Lost State of Franklin.

Sevier was both eager to settle with North Carolina and reluctant to desert his more ardent followers in the land south of the French Broad River. By early autumn 1788, however, the governor of North Carolina, Samuel Johnston, had instructed Judge David Campbell to arrest Sevier on charges of treason. He refused, and the order was then given to Tipton, who no doubt relished the prospect of incarcerating his formerly treasonous adversary.

On October 10, 1788, after eight months, John Sevier surrendered peacefully to his foe John Tipton and was imprisoned. Sevier was to face trial on charges of treason against the State of North Carolina due to his central part in the formation and defense of the unlawful State of Franklin. He was charged with having levied troops to oppose North Carolina's government and of killing good citizens with an armed force. Sevier refused to believe his actions were anything but heroic. Sevier's friend, General Charles McDowell, a fellow veteran commander at the Battle of King's Mountain, signed his bail bond. Later, as arrangements for his trial were being made, Sevier's sons and many friends were allowed to liberate him without interference. No trial was ever held.

Sevier, in the absence of any opposition, continued behaving as though the State of Franklin existed. For example, on January 12, 1789, he wrote to the "privy council of the State of Franklin" reporting that "the arms of Franklin gained complete victory over the forces of the Creeks and Cherokees on the 10th instant." According to his report:

> Our artillery…roused the Indians from their huts; and, finding themselves pretty near surrounded on all sides, they only tried to save themselves by flight, from which they were prevented by our riflemen posted behind the

trees...The battle soon became general...death presented itself on all sides in shocking scenes, and in less than half an hour the enemy ceased making resistance, and left...the bloody field.

The loss of the enemy...[was] 145...dead...Our loss is very inconsiderable...five dead and sixteen wounded; amongst the latter is the brave Gen. Carter, who, while taking of the scalp of an Indian was tomahawked by another whom he afterward killed...I am in hopes this brave and good man will survive.

Fighting Indians for the State of Franklin notwithstanding, on February 1789, John Sevier took the oath of allegiance to North Carolina. The State of Franklin was no longer moribund but expired and lost forever.

John Sevier, the governor of the Lost State of Franklin, would go on to become Tennessee's first governor on March 30, 1796. He would serve six two-year terms, from 1796 to 1801 and from 1803 to 1809. As governor, he negotiated with the Indian nations to secure their lands, opened new wagon roads and encouraged migration into Tennessee. However, he eschewed forever any notions of secession, ideas that would become potent politically in a mere sixty-five years and result in a much larger, deadlier war.

2
TENNESSEE'S ANDREW JACKSON AND THE EXPANSION OF DEMOCRACY

THE JOURNEY TO THE WHITE HOUSE, 1824–1828

The moribund Republican Party of Thomas Jefferson, the scourge of the Federalists, had by 1820 failed to maintain its organizational distinctions. At the same time, a rising dissatisfaction with arcane congressional caucus procedures as a means of choosing a presidential candidate left most of the nominations to the state legislatures and state nominating conventions because national nominating conventions were not yet a part of the American political process. Prospective nominees were quick to declare their intentions after James Monroe's victory in 1820. John C. Calhoun, President Monroe's secretary of war (1820–24), who had long harbored loftier political ambitions, was the first to announce his candidacy early in 1821. The Tennessee state legislature in Murfreesboro nominated Andrew Jackson on July 20, 1822, while John Quincy Adams was chosen by a meeting in Boston on February 18, 1822. On February 14, 1822, 66 percent of what was left of the National Republican Party held a rump congressional caucus and nominated Monroe's secretary of the treasury, William H. Crawford of Georgia, the last to be named as a presidential candidate.

A paralytic stroke virtually eliminated Crawford's candidacy in September 1823, and John C. Calhoun became the vice-presidential candidate on both the Adams and Jackson tickets. Although he did not take part in trading for votes, Adams held the strongest position, and he was able to profit by the division among the candidates from the South and West, Jackson and Clay. Adams's support for the "American System" brought him closer to

Engraved portrait of President John Quincy Adams.

Clay, who had vigorous disagreements with Tennessee's Jackson. Most of the candidates supported a strong system of protective tariffs and internal improvements. Jackson attacked these issues and continued to attack "King Caucus" as a means by which the people were prohibited from directly participating in the election of their own president.

In the end, the four-way contest was sent to the House of Representatives. Jackson had won 99 electoral votes, Adams 84, Crawford 41 and Clay 37. Jackson had won 152,933 popular votes. Adams 115,696, Clay 47,136 and Crawford 46,979. Clay was eliminated because of his low electoral vote count, and the election in the House of Representatives was now between the three remaining candidates. Disobeying its state legislature's instructions to vote for Jackson and acting under Clay's influence, the Kentucky delegation voted for Adams. The House vote of February 9, 1825, saw Adams receive the vote of thirteen states, while Jackson received the vote of seven and Crawford four. John Quincy Adams was elected the sixth president of the United States.

Soon after the House decision, in an unsigned letter to a newspaper by a Jackson supporter, Pennsylvania representative George Kremer accredited Adams's election to a "corrupt bargain," a charge that would gain more and more credence after Clay was appointed secretary of state. The charge would be repeated in 1827, when Andrew Jackson began his second campaign for the presidency. While most historians hold to the view that there is no compelling affirmation of the "corrupt bargain" assertion, it defamed Clay's name throughout his political career. The election of Adams, and the subsequent popular belief in the "corrupt bargain" charge, split the National Republican Party into two factions.

By October 1825, Jackson had resigned from the U.S. Senate after the Tennessee state legislature (then at Murfreesboro) nominated him for the presidency, and he began to build his support for the election in 1828. Jackson's election campaign was planned and managed by an accomplished group of newspaper editors and professional politicians, including James Buchanan, John H. Eaton of Tennessee, Duff Green, Amos Kindall and William B. Lewis. "Old Hickory" was extolled as a symbol of the common man, a frontier military hero and, in an about face from the 1824 campaign, as a supporter of the so-called American System.

The National Republican Convention at Harrisburg, Pennsylvania, nominated Adams for a second term with Richard Rush from Pennsylvania as his running mate. The Jacksonians, now the Democrats, based their crusade not on public issues but on personal grounds, and the National Republicans

Portrait of Andrew Jackson.

reciprocated in kind. The "corrupt bargain" charge was deadly as applied to Adams and Clay. The election of 1828 is unique for a number of reasons, as was the electioneering conducted during the campaign. In a sense, the modern presidential campaign with its negative ads was born in 1828.

Since the Democrats urged candidates to look to the people for support, they launched, according to Robert V. Rimini's classic work *The Election of Andrew Jackson*, "a novel campaign of song, slogan, and shout. In the process they inaugurated some of the worst barbarisms of American electioneering, but they also advanced the cause of democracy in the country, whether intended or not."

American voters, sometimes characterized as "pugnaciously unreflective," in general respond to stimulation more often than they think profoundly about political matters—the bigger the voter response, the greater the stimulation that has provoked it. The "Jackson men," from congressmen to state political leaders, journalists and stump orators, "were about to create a monumental stimulation—the first kind in presidential politics—and the degree to which the voters responded to it measured the extent of Old Hickory's victory in 1828." Gimmicks, Democrats found, worked better than reasoned argument to capture the vote. Accordingly, they resorted to tactics such as dinners, jokes, mass demonstrations, cartoons, propaganda, barbecues and hickory tree plantings, which were sure to generate widespread enthusiasm for Jackson.

It wasn't so much that Jackson was inaccurately touted as the symbol of the common man, the candidate of everyday people, but just as much that Adams was portrayed negatively as an aristocrat. An anglophobic America bristled at the alleged English affectations of President Adams. Even worse, the originator of the American System, Secretary Clay, "used English writing paper in the State Department!" The victor at the Battle of New Orleans, however, did not share this fondness for the English.

The Jacksonians utilized a variety of tactics to appeal to the several nationalities in America, some of them well thought out and aboveboard while others could not be so characterized. For example, they reminded immigrants that John Adams was the famous "creator" of the unconstitutional Alien and Sedition Acts of 1798. Jackson supporters, while campaigning in Pennsylvania, New Jersey and New York, convinced voters that supporters of the Adams coalition had "spoken of the Dutch [i.e., Germans], calling them 'the Black Dutch,' 'the Stupid Dutch,' 'the Ignorant Dutch,' and other names." Andrew Jackson, naturally enough, cherished the Dutch for their sturdy habits, patriotism and other republican virtues. To win the German vote in Pennsylvania, the Jacksonians published pamphlets, handbills and tracts in German. German-speaking lawyers were sent into the heavily populated German communities to hold public meetings and organize Jackson rallies. They lambasted the president for his alleged extravagance, treachery, corruption and support of higher taxes, and they achieved such a tremendous success in the Keystone State that long after his death, even after the Civil War, Pennsylvania Germans were reportedly still voting for Jackson.

Jackson was proclaimed an Irishman in Boston, and Democratic Party operatives held him up as the champion of the poor against the rich. In New York, De Witt Clinton, a favorite of the Irish community and a Jackson man, reminded his fellow Irishmen that to vote for Jackson was a patriotic duty. He did such a good job of stimulating his constituents that some one thousand illegal ballots would supplement the Hero of the Battle of New Orleans' total votes in New York returns in 1828.

To all those who treasured the recollection of the mighty British retreating before an army of aroused American farmers protecting their homeland, the Hero of the Battle of New Orleans was portrayed as a second George Washington. Jackson, the soldier lad of the Revolution, savagely scarred by a British officer, redeemed his honor and that of the nation with his stunning victories in the War of 1812. When Adams's coalition papers drew attention to Jackson's execution of American militiamen, the Democrats, more in tune with American Anglophobia, answered: "Jackson coolly and deliberately put to death upward of fifteen hundred British troops on the 8th of January, 1815, for no other offense than that they had wished to sup in the city that night."

Such propaganda aided the Democrats to identify Old Hickory with the array of American voters and encouraged many to vote the Democratic ticket. Soon, however, this approach was augmented with other novel electioneering practices, namely tricks and gimmicks that helped give the election of 1828 its unique place in Tennessee and American history. American voters were unprepared for some of the stunts initiated during the campaign, but after the first surprise had been dispensed, they desired more.

Perhaps the shrewdest and earliest move made by the Democrats was to adopt a symbol to represent their candidate. Since Jackson was already known as Old Hickory, the selection of a symbol was apparent. Almost immediately, hickory sticks, hickory brooms and hickory canes appeared across the nation, in the hands of children, on steamboats, at crossroads and on church steeples. Hickory poles were erected in many villages and at the corners of city streets, some remaining standing as late as 1845. Local militia companies and Jackson Clubs arranged public ceremonies to plant hickory trees in town and village squares as part of the crusade to enlighten the public mind. While the opposition press sarcastically asked what these hickory tree cultivation ceremonies had to do with the election, the Democrats did not stop planting them to let the Adams forces know.

Nearly as effective a technique was the organization of mass public rallies to honor the hero in New England, the Mid-Atlantic and the West. A "Grand Barbeque" was arranged by Robert B. Taney (later a Supreme Court chief justice) in Baltimore. The rally was held on the anniversary of Baltimore's defense against the British during the War of 1812. The celebration began with cannon firing, followed by a parade. Afterward, the crowd drank freely and toasted Jackson, the Hero of New Orleans. When the speeches telling of Jackson's thrilling victories ended, the assembled revelers sang a song called

"Hickory Wood" before eating. In 1827, the Fourth of July was utilized as a means to produce a pro-Jackson rally in New York: "Barbeques were advertised where the voters were told they could eat beef and pork and swill hard liquor 'under the shadow of a hickory bush.'" Southern Democrats followed suit in arousing the voters' interest in Jackson. According to one southerner: "Considerable pains were taken to bring out the people...flags were made and sent to different parts of the country, and the people came in companies of fifty or sixty with the flag flying at the head, with the words 'Jackson and Reform,' on it in large letters." The Democratic Party message was getting out.

Neither Jackson nor Adams campaigned often in person, the prevailing view being that it was undignified and improper to make personal appearances. Jackson, however, did make a tour to New Orleans to celebrate the anniversary of his victory over the British in what was billed as a nonpolitical trip. Accompanying the general on board the steamship *Pocahontas* were his closest Volunteer State advisors, including "Nashville Junto" members Judge John Overton, John Coffee, Sam Houston and William Carroll, along with deputations from a number of states. The Tennessee hero's welcome was tumultuous, including surging crowds, artillery blasts, toasts, dinners and rounds of huzzahs. Jackson's trip also brought Louisiana into the Democratic fold. The professional politicians of the Democratic Party Central Committee complimented themselves on having successfully conceptualized and arranged for so unique a political publicity exploit. Jackson rallies continued to be held, although without Old Hickory, who remained at his plantation home, the Hermitage. Nevertheless, such tactics were both novel and successful, and the people could learn more about the general. Adams's coalitionist forces referred to those who attended such public demonstrations as rabble, which only tended to make Tennessee's "Old Hickory" appear less aristocratic and more as having democratic sentiments.

For the first time in American political history, Democrats took opinion polls to promote Tennessee's favorite son. Grand juries, bridal parties, readers of certain newspapers, militias and others were all requested to state their selections in the presidential race. Once the results were published in the network of Democratic newspapers, politicians quickly realized that polls served the useful purpose of indicating the directions in which voters were leaning.

Early in the campaign, Democratic Party leaders were impressed with the pleasure with which the people had reacted to this completely trailblazing form of electioneering. The barbecues, rallies and tree plantings entertained

them and created a favorable impression of Tennessee's "Old Hickory."
Political campaign songs were sung at barbecues and rallies, such as
"The Battle of New Orleans" (sung to the tune of "Hail to the Chief"),
or "Hickory Wood." Even special political clothing was ushered in and
included hats decorated with hickory leaves, hickory walking canes, vests
and hickory buttons. All these devices indicated the wearer's allegiance to
General Jackson.

All these new campaign tactics resulted in a victory for the Democrats,
placing the first of Tennessee's three presidents in the Oval Office. The
Democrats, in seeking and winning popular campaigning, increased
newspaper coverage of the campaign. The use of songs, jokes, gimmicks,
mass demonstrations and blatant distortions advanced—even if
surreptitiously—the cause of democracy in America. Tennessee's Andrew
Jackson became the seventh president of the United States on the basis
of his personality, reputation on the battlefield and the notion that he was
the epitome of the American self-made man, regardless of his complete
inexperience in government. Yet with all these admirable attributes, his
election might never have been achieved without the aid of a capable and
professional political organization and media network that made Jackson's
qualities all the more alluring to the common man while disparaging those
of Adams. In the future, the availability of a candidate of the presidency
would rely less on his expertise in government and in larger measure on
his personal charisma and campaign organization. In fact, the Whig Party
successfully utilized the very same tactics in the "Log Cabin and Hard Cider"
campaign of 1840. It may not have been the intention of the outstanding
coterie of politicians who catapulted Tennessee's Andrew Jackson to the
presidency to advance democracy, but in the end, their tactics involved a
wider number of citizens in politics and so advanced the cause of American
participatory politics in Tennessee and the United States.

3
GRIDLOCK AND SECESSION

THE "IMMORTAL THIRTEEN" AND THE LEGISLATIVE DRIVE FOR THE CREATION OF FRANKLAND AND JACKSONIANA, 1841–1842

The defeat of Democrat James K. Polk and the election of Whig James Chamberlain "Lean Jimmy" Jones as governor of Tennessee in 1840 was accompanied by the return of a Whig majority in the House of Representatives. Democrats held a slim margin in the Senate with thirteen of twenty-five seats. It was a situation made for gridlock, and the Democratic senate majority, or the "Immortal Thirteen," took full advantage of it.

One of the most pressing pieces of business before the legislature was the selection of two United States senators. Both seats were unfilled. Felix Grundy (Democrat) died a few weeks after his November 1840 appointment, and Alfred Osborne Pope Nicholson (Democrat) was selected to hold his place until the legislature could choose a successor. Addison Alexander Anderson's (Whig) term expired on March 3, 1841.

The Whigs were assured that they could elect both senators because the conventional manner of electing such federal officials was by a special meeting of both houses of the entire General Assembly. Their majority in the House would thus give them control over the selection process. The slim Democratic majority in the Senate concluded that it would be in the party's best interest to have the election held separately in each house. In that way they need not cower before the Whig majority in the House and could then compel the Whigs to compromise by naming one Whig and one Democrat to the vacant federal posts. Both Whigs and Democrats in the Senate were adamant in their stance on the issue, the Whigs gaining the sobriquet the "Twelve Destructives" and the Democrats the "Immortal

Portrait of Felix Grundy.

Thirteen." One result of the gridlock was that there were no U.S. senators elected, so the Volunteer State remained unrepresented in the upper house of Congress until 1843. Blame was generally put on the "Immortal Thirteen," although the venerable former president Andrew Jackson believed the Democrats had preserved fundamental principles of American democracy by their actions. Democrats claimed to be protecting the rights of the minority while Whigs loudly protested that the will of the people was being ignored by the Democrats. According to Robert E. Corlew: "Successful in blocking the election of senators, the thirteen Democrats then resolved to obstruct other Whig legislation." For example, the "Immortal Thirteen" blocked Governor Jones's appointment of a new board of directors for the state bank, as well as an investigation into the affairs of the bank. Another way in which the "Immortal Thirteen" practiced their tactics resulted in one of the oddest and more comical

Portrait of Andrew Johnson.

episodes in Tennessee's political history. In the midst of the senatorial situation, the Democratic senator from Greene County, Andrew Johnson, on December 7, 1841, introduced a resolution:

> *That there be a joint committee appointed, to consist of two members on the part of the Senate, and three on the part of the House…whose duty it shall be to take into consideration the expediency and constitutionality of ceding one of the grand divisions of the State (commonly called East Tennessee) to the General Government, for the purpose of being formed into a sovereign and independent State, to be called "the State of Frankland."*

The resolution further called on Governor Jimmy Jones to open correspondence with the governors of Georgia, Virginia and North

Portrait of Governor James "Lean Jimmy" Jones.

Carolina to have their legislators consider the notion and to give their opinions about ceding part of their territory to Washington, D.C., in order that those lands might be added to the domain of the proposed "State of Frankland." The resolution remained quiescent until January of the next year. It is difficult to ascertain whether Johnson was serious about the suggested secession of East Tennessee from the Volunteer State. Perhaps he used the idea as a means to test both Democratic and Whig Party strength. In any event, whether he was earnest in his expressed prospects, a number of newspaper editors appeared to be nearly rapturous about the "Frankland" proposition. The secession movement apparently led to the submission of a second and no less audacious scheme by another of the "Immortal Thirteen," Senator John A. Gardner, who represented Obion, Weakley and Henry Counties. On December 15, 1841, he proposed that another joint legislative committee be established:

Whose duty it shall be to take into consideration, the expediency and constitutionality of ceding that portion of this State lying west of the Tennessee River, commonly called the Western District, to the…United States, for the purpose of being formed into a separate, independent and sovereign State to be called Jacksoniana.

Governor Jones was required to enter into correspondence with the governors of Mississippi and Kentucky in order to obtain parts of those states' territories for the proposed Jacksoniana.

Both secession proposals had been made by Democrats. Whether they were serious is unknown, but the anxious and anti-secessionist editor of the *Nashville Whig*, that party's organ for Middle Tennessee, seemed gravely threatened by the resolutions. According to the December 17, 1841 number of the newspaper:

Mr. Johnson from East Tennessee and Mr. Gardner from the Western District have each introduced resolutions in the Senate to dismember the State of Tennessee for the purpose of erecting two separate, sovereign, and independent states by adding portions of North Carolina and Georgia to the eastern division and by adding portions of Kentucky and Mississippi to the western. The first is to be called by the euphonic name of the "State of Frankland" and the second the "State of Jacksoniana." These projects of division, we believe, are seriously entertained but what are the advantages to be derived have not yet been explained as the resolutions have not yet been taken up by the Senate. Would not the movers of these resolutions render greater service to their country by reconsidering them and their ill-defined notions on constitutional law, and electing Senators to represent a State already organized, than by attempting the formation of a new state?

Two weeks later, the editor of the *Nashville Whig* combined satire and travesty in a column entitled "The State of Jacksoniana." According to the article:

The same reasons which have been urged in favor of the new State of Frankland may be made to apply to the formation of the new State of Jacksoniana. With power equal to that of the Senator from Greene [County] will the Senator from Weakley proclaim the advantages the Western District will derive from becoming a free, sovereign, and independent state? His fancy has no doubt, suggested to him that "westward the star of the empire takes its way," and his imagination has already pictured to him the star of Jacksoniana adding luster to the "Star Spangled Banner." Some of the good people of the district object to the name but such as object can have no poetry in their souls. Jacksoniana! How poetical the name! It falls as sweetly upon the ear as the gentle murmur of the rivulet on a summer's eve! Why did the Senator from Greene adopt the prosaic name of Frankland? Why did he not give it the more sonorous and poetical name of Franklandiana? We would suggest to him, when his resolutions are called up, to move to amend that he may be even with his associate from Weakley [County].

The editor of the Whig newspaper the *Knoxville Post* also took the matter of Frankland seriously but offered an opinion that differed markedly from his Middle Tennessee counterpart. The December 22, 1841 number of the editor of the *Post* exuberantly wrote:

We ardently hope that the members from this section of the State will press the subject at an early day upon the consideration of the Legislature. We are fully impressed with the belief that no sincerer objection to the proposed division will be made by Middle and West Tennessee, for a moment's reflection must convince everyone that it would conduce to the permanent happiness and prosperity of both. Our interests are so notoriously dissimilar, and the causes which produce this dissimilarity so entirely beyond human control, that a separation must be regarded as a mutual blessing, unless (which is hardly probable), the Seat of Government should be removed to East Tennessee.

The only impediment to the successful conclusion of the secessionist scheme was that part of Johnson's resolution that called for annexing parts of Georgia, Virginia and North Carolina. It would take "half a lifetime" to conclude the matter that way, so it would be best to let "the simple naked question of ceding back East Tennessee to the General Government, be the only one brought before the Legislature." Excitement among the people of East Tennessee was high, and even if Frankland could not be made a reality it would be better to be a territory of the United States government, "a much more desirable position…than to be tacked on merely as an appendage to the State of Tennessee, without participating in the blessings of good government." In summation, the Knoxville editor urged "our East Tennessee members to press the separation, and press it now. This is a more favorable time than will ever occur again, and if this opportunity is permitted to pass by, the object may never be accomplished." The editor of the *Knoxville Argus* argued in much the same vein and thought it best for "Col. Johnson" to remove that section of the resolution concerning the territory of adjoining states. Regional jealousies were evident in his remark that the "interests of East and West Tennessee are entirely distinct—East Tennessee wished to set up for herself, and the people west of the mountains have all along declared that we were a burden to them. Let them now consent to the almost unanimous wish of our people, who are not only willing, but anxious to rid them of the evil." On January 18, 1842, Johnson's "Frankland Resolution" was debated in the Senate. According to the *Nashville Whig* of January 20, the senator from Greene County waxed nostalgic and defended his idea saying:

> *The resolution was offered in good faith, and he wished to deliver a vote of the Senate on the subject. The project, he said, did not originate with him; the people of East Tennessee were in favor of it and it was a matter in which they manifested much interest. Mr. Johnson then proceeded and in a speech of about an hour in length stated the reasons which, in his opinion, rendered the separation of the Eastern from the Middle and Western Divisions of the State, proper and expedient. In the course of his remarks Mr. Johnson spoke of the Republican simplicity of the people of East Tennessee and adverted to the period when that part of the State formed a kind of separate sovereignty within the State of North Carolina* [i.e., the State of Franklin, 1784–88], *and when the people paid their taxes, and the public officers received their salaries in tow linen, maple sugar, beaver and raccoon skins and other commodities of the same kind. Mr. Johnson said the object of the people was to form just another simple Republican Democratic Government.*

His yearnings for the good old days were on their way to becoming reality when the resolution passed in the Senate on January 18 by a vote of seventeen to six. Thus, elements of the "Immortal Thirteen" and the "Twelve Destructives" could reach consensus to agree on something. The resolution was sent to the House of Representatives for concurrence. By January 21, the Senate was informed that the House of Representatives had approved of the Frankland issue but had amended the resolution to read: "Be it Further Resolved that the portion of East Tennessee comprised in the Ocoee and Hiwassee District shall not constitute a part of the State of Frankland without the consent of the people of said District."

Most likely this action did not get to Knoxville for several days, as the following optimistic observation of the secession movement appeared in the *Knoxville Argus* five days after the January 21 rider had been attached. In retrospect, the editorial reads more like the editor's pipe dream than reality:

> *We continue to look upon the creation of a separate, sovereign State out of the territory comprised within the limits of East Tennessee, as of the very first importance to our citizens. It would do more to unshackle the enterprise of our people than any thing [sic] else... True, we would be but a small State at first—yet not smaller than several of our sisters—and, with our vast resources and natural advantages, who can doubt that our wealth and population would advance with a rapidity unexampled in the history of the most prosperous States of the confederacy? Disenthral [sic] us from the degrading position we occupy as a province dependent upon Nashville, and an impulse will be given to the enterprise of our citizens which would speedily place our new State among the first agricultural and manufacturing districts of the Union. Our unlimited water power will be called into use; our inexhaustible mines will be worked; roads will be opened to the best markets; and our noble rivers, instead of lazily rolling their way in silence to the ocean, will be enlivened by the busy hum of commerce.*

Senator Johnson successfully, if not intentionally, put the entire matter to rest on January 25 when he moved that the Senate refuse to accept the House amendment. The suggested West Tennessee state likewise suffered a final defeat when Senator Gardner brought up his resolution on February 2. Short shrift was made of the suggestion, and by a vote of fourteen to eleven, the proposed state of Jacksoniana was stopped dead in its tracks. The very next day, however, Johnson introduced a resolution to move the state capital permanently to Knoxville. It may well have been that Johnson was shoring up his political capital by testing the political waters in his region of the state with his apparently ridiculous resolutions. The issue of the location of the capital was an emotionally charged one in the Volunteer State ever since 1796. His Frankland resolution likewise played on this sectional question. Perhaps in so doing he found a "hot button" topic with which to further his own political ambitions.

A number of circumstances played roles in decisively defeating this secession movement: a common sense perspective of a substantial number of members of the legislature who were convinced such impulsive undertakings merited frustration; the Whig House of Representatives that rejected the Frankland notion and the divided Senate that turned down the Jacksoniana resolution offered by members of the Democratic "Immortal Thirteen" Senators Johnson and Gardner; the lack of unity among Middle Tennessee and East Tennessee Whigs on the issue; and the objections of the Ocoee and Hiwassee districts to be included in the new state. Thus, the people of East and West Tennessee were thwarted from realizing a vision they hardly knew they shared. While the issue of secession would arise again in Tennessee in the 1850s and be made real in 1861, it was at that later date directed at separation of the Volunteer State from the Union, not from itself. Still, secession did not meet with universal approval, with East Tennessee largely against the notion that it championed in 1841–42.

4
WILLIAM WALKER

TENNESSEE'S GRAY-EYED FILIBUSTERER
OF MANIFEST DESTINY

Nicaragua, the Gold Rush of 1849, Cornelius "Commodore" Vanderbilt, Manifest Destiny, England's Royal Navy, the course of diplomacy and war in Central America in the late 1850s and Nashville all share a connection with one of the more mysterious, yet in his time, world-renowned Tennesseans in America's late antebellum era. Romantically called "the gray-eyed man of destiny" by his contemporaries, William Walker would earn distinctions of fame and infamy.

William's father, James, had emigrated from Scotland and arrived in Nashville in 1820 to receive an inheritance: a dry goods store. He soon married a daughter of the Novell family, Mary. Soon, James became the founder of a commercial insurance agency, and his first son, William, was born in Nashville on May 8, 1824. The stern spirit of Knox and Calvin played a significant role in William's youth, whose family were members of the Disciples of Christ church.

A superb student, he entered the University of Nashville at age twelve and graduated summa cum laude. To qualify for admission to the university was no modest undertaking. A student had to be well versed in *belles-lettres*, Latin and Greek, mathematics, calculus, history, oratory, philosophy, astronomy and natural history. Religion was also stressed at the university—prayers twice daily in chapel, church on Sundays and a long benediction at morning and evening meals. After graduating at age fourteen (1838), he attended the Medical College at the University of Pennsylvania, and in 1843, at age nineteen, he graduated with a medical degree. Instead of beginning a

WILLIAM WALKER, born in Nashville, was president of Nicaragua and was executed by the Honduran government at Truxillo, Hr duras, Sept. 12, 1860. He was known as "The Grey-Eyed Man of Destiny."

Photographic portrait of William Walker, the "gray-eyed filibusterer of destiny."

practice, he traveled to Europe to continue his medical education, and then he returned to Nashville. Impatient with medical science, he was not to pursue a career as a physician. He opted, instead, for the law.

Traveling to New Orleans, Louisiana, he read the law, and by 1847, he was qualified to practice. Qualified but not interested, he abandoned the law to take a place on the editorial staff of the *New Orleans Crescent*. Soon after, his fiancée died tragically of cholera then raging in the city. At twenty-four years of age, Walker had already been a doctor, lawyer and newspaper editor. Another career would soon be pursued.

The year 1848 was a tumultuous one for the United States and for the world at large. By the Treaty of Guadalupe-Hidalgo, which ended the Mexican-American War, for example, the United States codified its possession, by force of arms, to nearly one-half of Mexico's lands in California, the Southwest and Texas. Also that year, gold was discovered in California, while the British were making incursions on the eastern shore of Nicaragua, known as the "Mosquito Coast." Cornelius Vanderbilt was likewise interested in the area. It was then strategically important as the shortest and fastest route between the eastern seaboard and the gold in California and was, many Americans agreed, destined to be under the control of the United States. "Manifest destiny" refers to the spirited belief that America was destined to install its democratic institutions everywhere throughout the Western Hemisphere. The Monroe Doctrine seemed somehow to similarly justify American interest in the isthmus. It was in these charged times that the "gray-eyed man of destiny" would follow the Forty-Niners and head for San Francisco.

In San Francisco, he found work as an editor for the *San Francisco Herald*, was wounded while fighting a number of duels and enthusiastically supported the work of Cornelius Vanderbilt. According to one of Walker's editorials: "The presence of the enterprising and indefatigable Commodore Vanderbilt will insure [*sic*] the perfection of all arrangements to make the transit connection (between the Atlantic and Pacific) complete." By 1851, Vanderbilt had completed the 119-mile course of the San Juan River and entered Lake Nicaragua and had thus established a lucrative transport business: the American Transit Company.

It was at this time that Walker, now twenty-seven years old, abruptly left San Francisco for a law practice in Marysville, California. In Marysville in 1852, Walker became interested in events in the Mexican province of Sonora, where a French company led by the soldier-of-fortune Count Gaston Raoul de Raousset-Gabson had begun to exploit mining possibilities. That spring, Walker formed a group to approach the provincial governor and to attempt to obtain permission to allow a few American colonists to immigrate to Sonora. The governor refused. The French company had overlooked the military commander of Sonora, General Miguel Blanco, in its stock distribution plan, which led a San Francisco banking house to successfully bribe him. Eventually, Blanco would resist a French-led "revolution," but Raousset-Gabson, who led the effort, returned to San Francisco to a hero's welcome.

Walker's interest in the Sonoran affair quickened, and by early 1850, he was in San Francisco to speak to Raousset and effect another try. The Frenchman refused, saying Americans were the most hated of all people in Mexico and thus would seriously hobble any such effort. Walker vowed then to invade and subdue Sonora independently. He would introduce a group of American "colonists" and seize power. Sonora would then be proclaimed an independent nation, and he would ask for the protection of the United States government and give mining concessions to an American company, fulfilling "manifest destiny." Funding was raised through the secret sale of bonds guaranteed by the value of the Sonoran land he would soon conquer.

In the Sonoran port city of Guaymas, Walker waited for word from the governor of the province to discuss the colonization matter. Spending his time with the small American colony there, he learned of alleged Apache depredations against American women. Fearing the governor had learned of his true intent, Walker hurried back to San Francisco to raise men and supplies for a military action to subdue the Apaches. His actions were successful, but on the last day of September 1853, the United States Army general in charge of San Francisco seized the ship, suspecting that it was to be utilized to violate the U.S. Neutrality Act. Unwilling to wait, Walker commissioned another brig, the *Caroline*, rounded up forty-five men and sailed, before they could be seized, on October 8, 1853.

Walker's motivation is probably best expressed by writer Albert Z. Carr, who holds that

> *Walker was being driven by idealism and ambition together—an irresistible combination when their thrust is in the same direction. He believed with all his heart that the democratic institutions of the United States offered hope to the peoples of the world and that there was an obligation on Americans to bring the light of democracy to their benighted neighbors. At the same time he held in his heart the heroic dream of world fame.*

His failure at his first attempt at conquest was not only complete but likewise absurd. Efforts went well initially, with the capture of the province's capital and the governor and Walker's proclamation that Sonora was now the "Republic of Lower California" and that he was its president. While his army fought well, his provisions, especially food, ran low. Meanwhile, in Mexico City, the American government, unknown to Walker, had been negotiating to buy northern Sonora. Believing that Walker had the backing of the United States, Mexican officials erroneously believed their options in regard to Sonora were now limited, and they agreed to sell. The result is known in American history as the Gadsden Purchase of 1853.

Now that the coveted mineral-bearing part of Sonora was transferred to America, the public largely lost interest in Walker's filibustering (Dutch for "freebooting") activities.

While some in the ranks availed themselves of his offer to leave, Walker remained in Sonora and marched through the desert to reach the Colorado River. On May 8, 1854, his thirtieth birthday, Walker and the thirty-four remaining in his force marched across the border into California. Charged with violation of American neutrality laws, Walker entered state politics as a delegate to the constitutional convention. It would be his only experience in practical American politics.

After the convention, he was busy with political journalism, and soon he was invited to join the editorial board of the *San Francisco Commercial-Democrat*, a post he accepted. His intense interest in Manifest Destiny was shared by the newspaper's owner, a wealthy New Englander, Byron Cole. Cole's journey to California had been through Nicaragua's abundance of natural resources, which made for an excellent opportunity.

The situation revived Walker's vision of extending the blessings of American democratic institutions. (Nicaragua was then engaged in a civil war between the "Democrats" and "Legitimists.") Regardless of American neutrality laws, or the Clayton Bulwer Treaty, the Nicaraguan Democrats deserved American support. Moreover, British collusion in the Nicaraguan civil war violated the Monroe Doctrine. While Walker saw heroic visions, Cole was down-to-earth. As owner of the Honduras Mining Company, he realized that if the Legitimists won in Nicaragua, Honduras would most likely fall to pro-British forces, and thus his interests would be endangered.

Early in 1855, Cole had obtained a signed contract offering land to Americans in exchange for serving in the army of the Democratic forces. After receiving unofficial notice that neutrality laws would not be enforced against him, on May 4, 1855, Walker sailed to Nicaragua with forty-eight mercenaries, "the immortals." Five months later, *La Falange Americana*, under Walker's reinforced command, had substantially helped in concluding the Democratic revolution; he was made commander in chief of the new coalition-provisional government. His popularity with the native population would subside, especially after executing a popular coalition general and acting on his plan to Americanize Nicaragua.

In his position, Walker was able to increase American immigration, which was aided by grants of Nicaraguan land. Estimates place the total number of American immigrants as high as eleven thousand. Colorful brochures on Nicaraguan agriculture, mineral deposits and land for colonists required a great deal of money. In New York, Vanderbilt, after returning from a successful social tour of Europe, found that his competitors, Charles Morgan and Cornelius K. Garrison, had nearly ruined his Nicaraguan steamship line, the Accessory Transit Company, through corporate fraud and dishonesty in Nicaragua. Walker soon accepted a deal from Vanderbilt's competitors in which the American Transit Company's charter would be revoked. The Nicaraguan government would then transfer the property to Morgan and Garrison, who would form their own transit company. Walker would receive benefits in the way of aid from the new company to aid him in his Americanization project. Vanderbilt wrote his famous terse letter to Morgan and Garrison, saying in part, "I will ruin you." Walker was included.

Each arriving boat of American colonists heightened Nicaraguan president Don Patrico Rivas's fear for his country. He looked for aid in case it became necessary to overthrow this "gray-eyed man of destiny." Neighboring states were likewise fearful and believed Walker would move to conquer all of Central America and formed a coalition army. Costa

Rica attacked Walker first, on February 27, 1856. Walker's deterrence of the attack helped in his non-contested election as president of the Republic of Nicaragua in June. In a bid to win the support of Southern immigrants, he reinstated the condition of slavery. Shortly thereafter, the combined forces of Guatemala, San Salvador, Honduras and Nicaraguan Legitimists attacked and occupied Managua. It was not long before Walker's forces, thinned by cholera and desertion, withdrew.

Cornelius Vanderbilt saw this situation as the means to ruin his competitors and William Walker. The "Commodore's agents armed the Costa Ricans against Walker, commandeered all American Transit property, and effectively closed the San Juan River, severely limiting Walker's communication and supply efforts. By May Day, 1857, Walker surrendered his army to U.S. Navy Commander Charles H. Davis, and boarded the U.S.S. *St. Mary.*"

Three weeks later, he landed in New Orleans to a tumultuous greeting and was even lifted to the crowd's shoulders and taken to a waiting carriage. Speaking to a mass meeting, he made no secret of his desire to return to Central America. During his speaking tour from Memphis to Cincinnati and to New York that summer, he stressed that Southern institutions should best be planted in Central America. He planned to return to Nicaragua to try a second time. By the fall of 1857, enough money had been raised so that Walker, again in violation of neutrality laws, sailed to Greytown, Nicaragua, with a force of 240 volunteers. Shortly after his landing, elements of the U.S. Navy demanded his surrender for violating the neutrality acts. He was carried back to the United States, where President James Buchanan and various senators castigated his filibustering activities. Undeterred and bolstered by a wave of Southern support, Walker planned a third *filibuster sortie* in the Central American Republic of Nicaragua.

In the fall of 1858, a force of 120 men left Mobile Bay without Walker, who stayed ashore to allay suspicion. The mission failed when their ship ran aground; the HMS *Basilisk* returned them to Mobile. Still unwilling or unable to give up, this Tennessean tried a fourth time and failed to even get out of port. He settled in Mobile and wrote his account of actions in Nicaragua, *The War in Nicaragua*, in 1860.

It was also in 1860 that the largely English population on the small island of Ruatan, off the east coast of Honduras, asked Walker for his help. England planned to cede the island back to the Central American Republic, an act the inhabitants refused to recognize. He accepted and soon had invaded Honduras and captured the customhouse and the old Spanish fortress of Truxillo. Walker declared it a free port. Soon, however, the HMS *Icarus* appeared, and its captain demanded that since the customs of the port were mortgaged to England for payment of debt due from Honduras, in seizing the customhouse and the collections in it, Walker had taken illegal possession of British property.

Facing overwhelming odds, Walker knew he could not hold the fort, and since surrender to the British was unthinkable, the Americans left under cover of night. Assailed by native attacks, his force, facing the inevitable, returned to Truxillo and surrendered to the British. In short order, Walker was turned over to the Honduran officials. On September 12, 1860, William Walker was marched to an old fortress outside the town and summarily executed by a Honduran firing squad. His burial plot is not marked. William Walker's story would be quickly forgotten as the Civil War diverted attention to more pressing and serious concerns. Nevertheless, William Walker's filibustering provided an example to help justify an American martial presence in Nicaragua when it was occupied by the United States Marine Corps in 1911–12 and in 1927–33. Most recently, in the 1980s, the contra policy serves as an example of continuity in American/Nicaraguan relations since the 1850s.

There are at least three monuments and one historic marker resulting from Walker's adventurism in Central America. In the small town of San Jacinto, Nicaragua, stands a statue of a youthful soldier, who, finding himself out of ammunition, dispatched one of Walker's forces with an energetically thrown rock; the young boy is revered by Nicaraguans as a symbol of the struggle against American filibustering. In the public square in San Jose, Costa Rica, is a commemorative statue expressing similar emotions. It depicts a severe-faced woman whose foot is on the neck of a fallen American filibusterer. She is held in high esteem for turning the tide of Costa Rica's battle with William Walker. In Truxillo, Honduras, is found what is reputed to be the concrete-covered tomb of William Walker.[1] (Years later, attempts to reinter his remains in Tennessee were denied by Honduran officials.)

In Nashville, Tennessee, is a marker erected by the Metropolitan Nashville/Davidson County Historical Commission at the northeast corner of Fourth Avenue North and Commerce Street in Nashville, which reads:

Born May 8, 1824, Walker moved to this site from 6th Ave. N., in 1840. In early life he was a doctor, lawyer, and journalist. He invaded Mexico in 1853 with 46 men and proclaimed himself Pres., Republic of Lower California. Led forces into Nicaragua in 1855; was elected its Pres. in 1856. In an attempt to wage war on Honduras, he was captured and executed Sept. 12, 1860.

5

TENNESSEE'S "GENERAL" JOHN HUGH ("JEHAZY") McDOWELL (1844–1927)

A CONDENSED BIOGRAPHY OF AN ERSTWHILE REBEL AND POLITICAL NONCONFORMIST

John Hugh McDowell, Confederate veteran, farmer, editor, legislator, reformer and quintessential Tennessee politician from 1880 until 1915, died on February 20, 1927, at his home in Memphis. He was eighty-three years old.

As one of McDowell's contemporaries, Edward W. Carmack observed, the general's politics frequently made it appear that consistency was the hobgoblin of small minds. But his military and political lives are a kaleidoscopic swath woven into the rich tapestry of late nineteenth- and early twentieth-century Tennessee politics.

John Hugh McDowell was born in Gibson County, near Trenton, in 1844. On May 10, 1861, he enlisted as a private in Russell's Twelfth Tennessee Infantry. He fought in one of the first Civil War battles in which Tennesseans were engaged: Belmont, Missouri, November 7, 1861. He fought at Shiloh, and after the evacuation of Corinth, Mississippi, he joined Captain W.W. McDowell's (his older brother) company. He remained with his brother, serving the unit as sergeant. McDowell participated in the Battles of Iuka and Corinth. He participated in a daring night attack on Holly Springs, Mississippi, which caused General U.S. Grant to abandon his first Vicksburg campaign. In the Holly Springs engagement, McDowell told of his experience when two Federal troopers were ordered to separate Captain McDowell from his company. One rode headlong through the Confederate line, slashing right and left with his saber, but was soon killed and fell with six bullets in his body. The Sharps rifle the Illinoisan carried was given to

Sergeant McDowell, who carried it for the duration and treasured it after the war. Another episode the general related was his time with General Earl Van Dorn's cavalry at Thompson Station, Tennessee, on March 5, 1863. While he was scouting in the direction of Franklin, he was told of a Wisconsin captain and thirteen privates who had escaped from the battle and were hiding in a brick house. He demanded their surrender. The Yankees quickly complied, and McDowell marched them back to headquarters. After the death of General Van Dorn, McDowell's company was reassigned to General Tyree Harris Bell's escort, Jackson's division, Forrest's cavalry corps. He participated in some forty engagements, including the retreat from Vicksburg to Meridian, the Hundred Days' campaign in Georgia and

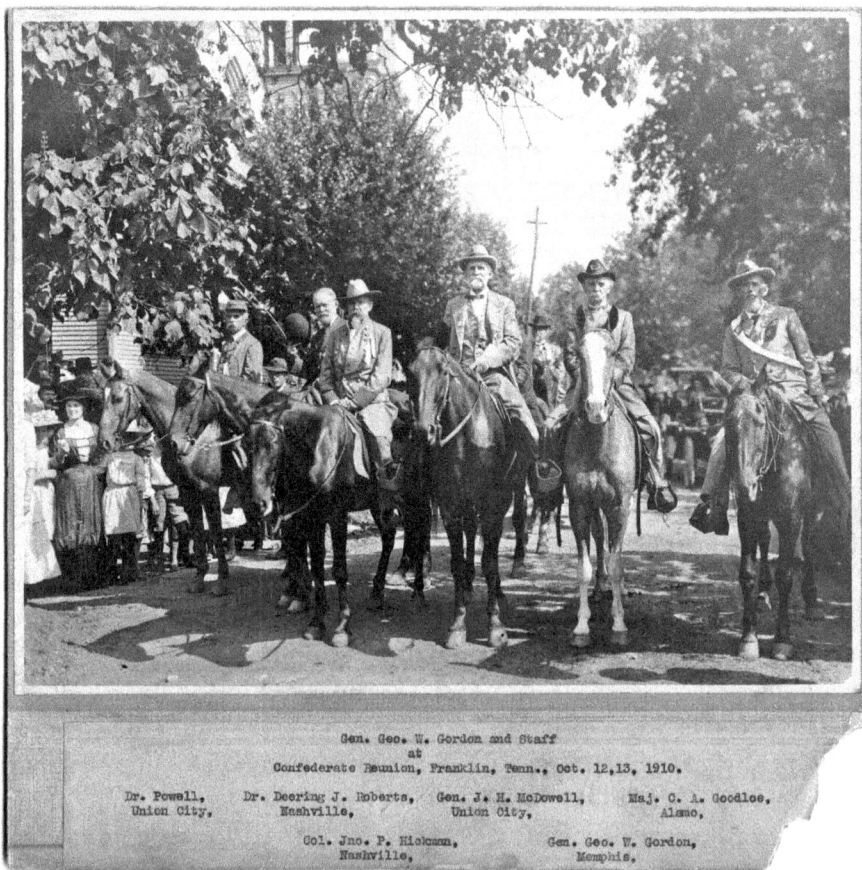

Gen. Geo. W. Gordon and Staff
at
Confederate Reunion, Franklin, Tenn., Oct. 12,13, 1910.

Dr. Powell, Union City, Dr. Deering J. Roberts, Nashville, Gen. J. H. McDowell, Union City, Maj. C. A. Goodloe, Alamo,

Col. Jno. P. Hickman, Nashville, Gen. Geo. W. Gordon, Memphis.

General J. Gordon and staff at a Confederate reunion at Franklin in 1910. McDowell is astride his horse, second from the right.

Hood's disastrous campaign in Tennessee. He served just over four years with the Army of Tennessee.

Within a few months after his discharge, he went home and married. During the Reconstruction period, the McDowells moved to the Arkansas delta. In 1876, they moved to Obion County, where McDowell became a successful farmer.

The general's political career began in the Forty-third General Assembly (1883–85) as the representative for Obion County, and he served in the state senate in the Forty-fourth and Forty-fifth General Assemblies (1885–89), representing Dyer, Lake and Obion Counties. He was nominally a Democrat. His first act was to have passed a law forbidding the playing of baseball on Sunday afternoons. He believed the law would prevent youngsters from abandoning their Sunday school lessons and betting on the games. He insisted that baseball teams should, like all businesses, be forbidden to operate on Sundays.

Temperance forces and strong support from farmers advanced McDowell into politics in 1883. He was at first a stalwart Democrat. Throughout his career in the Forty-third to Forty-fifth General Assemblies, he fought the whiskey interests. Yet he took time to refute charges made against the Governor William B. Bate (1883–87) wing of the party, namely that it was controlled by the "whiskey rings."

In 1885, as senator from Obion County, McDowell succeeded in passing an antigambling bill. As a member of the Prohibitionist wing of the Democratic Party, he worked to bring a constitutional amendment to the people to outlaw the manufacture and sale of alcoholic beverages in the state. It was not until the gubernatorial election of 1888 that the electorate decided the question. Although he had strong prohibitionist views, he remained within the Democratic fold. He argued that nothing would be achieved by voting for the Prohibition Party candidate. Every vote for them was a vote for the Republican Party. Democrat Robert L. Taylor won the election, which was a defeat for prohibition.

In the 1870s and 1890s, political discontent arose in the West and in the South. It was sequentially called the Grange, the Agricultural Wheel, the Farmers' Alliance and, finally, the People's (or Populist) Party. McDowell would play a significant role in this swell of agrarian protest. He owned and edited the Tennessee Farmers' Alliance journal the *Weekly Toiler*. It became the official organ of the Alliance and People's Party in Tennessee. McDowell also served as secretary, executive board member president of the Tennessee Alliance and vice-president of the Southern Alliance.

In Tennessee, the Alliance worked within the Democratic Party. In this way, the Alliance played a major role in the election of Democrat John P. Buchanan as governor in 1890. The Tennessee Democratic Party was divided into three factions: the Alliance, or "wool hat boys"; the "New South" element led by robber baron A.S. Colyar; and the "Bourbons," or "machine" faction led by U.S. senator Isham G. Harris, Tennessee's erstwhile Confederate governor. The Bourbons had controlled the party since 1870.

There were seven candidates for the Democratic nominee for governor. The strongest were the railroad man Jere Baxter, the Bourbon favorite Josiah Patterson and the Alliance preference John P. Buchanan. The *Nashville American* and the *Memphis Scimitar* both backed Patterson. McDowell supported John P. Buchanan, who was a Tennessee Farmers' Alliance member and president of the combined statewide Wheel and Alliance. Buchanan could absolutely count on the Alliance Democrats because McDowell, president of the state Farmers' Alliance, was his campaign manager. By way of Alliance meetings and the pages of the *Weekly Toiler*, McDowell urged farmers not to vote for "scheming politicians" but for Buchanan, friend to the farmer.

Working from the bottom up, McDowell's machine won a majority of the county conventions and instructed Alliance delegates to the state Democratic convention to back Buchanan. Buchanan won the nomination unanimously after twenty-six ballots. The "wool hat boys" were unbridled in their enthusiasm. It was reported in the *Weekly Toiler* that McDowell was so excited that "he lost his senses and his hat in hilarious rejoicing." There was so much disorder and confusion that, according to the *Knoxville Journal*, in contrast, "the playground of the insane asylum would be like an old maid's seven o'clock tea." McDowell crowed in the *Weekly Toiler* that the "shrewdest politicians in the state, trained for years in political wire pulling, have been out-witted…in a fair…fight…they have gracefully…fallen into line with a will that inspires perfect harmony in the Democratic party."

The Democrats faced the Republican nominee, Lewis T. Baxter, and the Prohibitionist Party candidate. The Farmers' Alliance nominated Buchanan, the Democratic nominee. Under McDowell's guidance, Buchanan won the Alliance vote and the election.

Motivated by his triumph over the Bourbons in 1890, McDowell wasted little time in organizing for another victory in 1892. His organizational work, however, was seriously complicated by the appearance of the People's Party, which he joined. The Bourbons wasted little time in repudiating McDowell and Buchanan as renegades in an unvarnished bid for power. After this, he could no longer work from within the Democratic Party.

Governor Buchanan ran a conservative administration, of which the Bourbons approved, but the governor's pro-business settlement of the Coal Creek War in 1891–92 left him little public support. It was the Bourbon, not the Alliance, wing of the Democratic Party that was slighted concerning patronage matters. Few Bourbons but many Alliance Democrats found valuable political appointments. For example, McDowell received a plum sinecure as "coal oil inspector" in Nashville.

McDowell was regarded by both parties, but especially by Bourbons, as a political loose cannon, a maverick and an upstart. His renewed efforts to control the Democratic Party and his aspiration to succeed United States senator William B. Bate (1887–1905) distressed the conservatives in the party. McDowell denied he was the least bit interested in the Senate seat. Nevertheless, the *Weekly Toiler* announced on October 19, 1892, "J.H. McDowell, the outspoken defender of the overburdened tax-payers, is the choice by general consent for the United States Senate by those who are honestly fighting for governmental reform."

The Bourbon press attacked McDowell. To defeat his bid for the Senate, the Bourbon press made him the mark of broadsides of editorial scorn, insult and reproach, unequaled in Tennessee journalism since the days of William G. Brownlow's *Whig*. The verbose and clever editor of the *Nashville American*, Edward W. Carmack, led the attack. It would be only natural, wrote Carmack, for McDowell to become U.S. senator because all knew "that God-Almighty never gave him that mass of storm stricken and [those] insurrectionarily [sic] whiskers and made him look like a weather beaten tintype of [a] Senator...for nothing...McDowell, noble knight of the horny hand and stone bruised heel, we, the played-out, Bourbon, moss-back, upper-case Democrats salute thee." Not only did Carmack and the Bourbon Democrats take to the hustlings to ridicule the entire Farmers' Alliance platform but they also used fear of black domination to fight the farmers' choice. In one of the more abusive attacks, it was said that while living in Arkansas during the Reconstruction period, McDowell was a member of the Republican "Loyal League." In this capacity, he closely fraternized with the newly enfranchised black citizens. It was even said that while in Arkansas he dined with one black man named Jehazy Cole. Soon, Carmack nicknamed him "Jehazy" McDowell—the sobriquet stuck with him until death. The Alliance leader retaliated by printing sworn notices from his erstwhile Razorback neighbors that denied the charges. He would face yet another more powerful challenge to his leadership of the Alliance wing of the Democratic Party.

McDowell continued to work for the renomination of Governor Buchanan, but his control of the Alliance Democrats was weakened by the appearance of the People's Party in 1891–92. The People's Party was established in St. Louis, Missouri, on February 22, 1892. McDowell initially opposed it, still hoping he could maintain control of the Tennessee Democratic Party by means of the Farmers' Alliance. As those hopes dimmed, he changed his mind and attended the St. Louis meeting. Upon his return, McDowell was faced with charges that he had abandoned the Democratic Party. While he denied the allegations, he worked to convene an assembly of Tennessee labor and Alliance leaders, called the State Labor Congress. In guiding this effort, McDowell tried to unite Tennessee's Alliancemen with urban labor forces in Tennessee, hoping for Governor Buchanan's renomination. In the end, the Bourbons nominated Judge Peter Turney.

Meanwhile, many Alliance Democrats had forsaken Buchanan and, following McDowell's lead, joined the People's Party. The first meeting of the new party was in Nashville, where delegates were chosen to attend the national party convention in Omaha, Nebraska. McDowell knew there were no prospects of reconciliation or alliance with the Democratic Party and so abandoned it. The Republicans, also plagued with division, nominated George W. Winstead.

Having lost control of the Democratic Party, McDowell's Populists endorsed the independent candidacy of Governor Buchanan. Knowing the Democrats were going into the election divided, the Republican Party was in a position to win the election if it could ally with the People's Party.

In the South, the election of 1892 was characterized by alliances between Republicans and Populists against Democrats in congressional and state races. This was true in Tennessee, too. During the campaign, Democrats discovered and printed the so-called Ivins-Hill correspondence. Jo J. Ivins, editor of the *Knoxville Republican*, carried on a correspondence with D.W. Hill, Tennessee's representative on the Republican national committee. The letters indicated that McDowell had taken a $15,000 payment in return for throwing Populist support behind the Republican candidate for governor. As quid pro quo, McDowell was assured election to the U.S. Senate. The charges were refuted by McDowell, who charged in the *Weekly Toiler*, "The Turney men are in a desperate strait and will resort to desperate means to carry out their concocted plans."

Dismay was not accurate enough a word to summarize the reaction to this political bombshell at Republican and Populist headquarters. The Democrats printed and distributed the correspondence, and the effect was disastrous for populist McDowell and the divided Republican Party. Democrat Peter Turney was elected.

McDowell had accompanied Populist presidential candidate General James B. Weaver (who served in Middle Tennessee during the Civil War) in his swing through the Volunteer State in October 1892. It was a risky venture, and McDowell felt compelled to carry a revolver in his pocket, due to Democratic harangues like that delivered by Carmack in Pulaski. In the midst of the confusion, McDowell was involved in the Eighth Congressional District contests of 1892 and 1894. In both instances, McDowell backed the Republican candidate, John E. McCall, over incumbent Democrat Benjamin Augustine Enloe. McDowell, the Confederate veteran, argued that Enloe had served in the Federal army during the Civil War. Inasmuch as Enloe was only thirteen when war broke out, the charge was absolutely false. The voters believed McDowell in the 1894 contest and elected McCall. Two years later, when William Jennings Bryan, "the great commoner," secured the support of the Populists and the Democrats for his presidential bid, McDowell supported the "silver-throated orator." After the Democratic-Populist defeat in 1896, he remained politically silent for the next decade.

McDowell was elected to the Fifty-fourth General Assembly representing Obion County from 1905 to 1907. McDowell, now a Democrat, supported the national party's candidate, Alton B. Parker, but not the state party's gubernatorial candidate, Malcom R. Patterson. As president of the Union City Anti-Saloon League, he, along with the Republicans, reprinted statements accusing Patterson of episodic public drunkenness in the election of 1906 (in July 1913, Patterson's career plummeted after his arrest in a Nashville brothel). Patterson won the election, serving two terms, from 1907 to 1911. Apparently, Patterson bore him no ill will, appointing McDowell state livestock inspector in 1907. During the election of 1908, McDowell rewarded Patterson's favor by supporting his old enemy Edward Carmack as the Democratic nominee for governor. Malcom Patterson won the nomination and the governor's chair. Soon, the general returned to his farm.

McDowell became ever more active in the affairs of the Tennessee Confederate Veterans Association. He had long been involved with the organization, serving as commander of the McDonald Camp, Union City, Colonel First Regiment Reserved Confederate Veteran National Guard State of Tennessee, 1897–99. He held several command positions with the Confederate Veterans in Memphis and as major general of the United Confederate Veterans of Tennessee, 1910–12. His political career seemed to have ended, but the general would step once more into the breach.

The year 1912 was one of political turbulence, noted in part for the formation of the Progressive (or "Bull Moose") Party, led by former president

Theodore Roosevelt. The presidential election that year was a three-way contest between the Democrat Woodrow Wilson, the Republican William H. Taft and the "Bull Moose" Theodore Roosevelt. The state's Democrats supported Wilson—all but McDowell. Roosevelt made a campaign trip to Memphis in late September. When Roosevelt arrived in the Bluff City (i.e., Memphis), he was seeking the votes of Tennessee's Confederate veterans. By his side stood John H. McDowell arrayed in the uniform of a Confederate major general. Asked if he would make any comments, Roosevelt replied, "No, General McDowell will talk for me." Roosevelt then deliberately asked McDowell: "By the way, General, when were you commander of the Confederate Veterans in Tennessee?" McDowell affectedly replied: "Why, I am now, sir, at this time, sir." Roosevelt said he was delighted. Quickly thereafter, Roosevelt was escorted to a waiting limousine by McDowell. The general accompanied Roosevelt the next day for a speech in Jackson, Tennessee, and no doubt most Confederate veterans were unimpressed. Woodrow Wilson won the election in the Volunteer State.

This last act of political activism on McDowell's part was not only his last but also would adversely influence his tenure as major general of the United Confederate Veterans of Tennessee. At the annual Confederate Veterans' Reunion at Shelbyville on October 2, 1912, General McDowell was accused of debasing his uniform in his appearance with Roosevelt. Ultimately, he was exonerated. Unlike his predecessor, Major General G.W. Gordon, who served in the leadership role from 1900 to 1910, McDowell was never again elected to the post. He stayed active with the Confederate Veterans in Memphis. It may or may not be significant that his passing was not mentioned in the *Confederate Veteran*, the journal of the Confederate Veterans. Perhaps the memory of "Jehazy" McDowell publicly backing Theodore Roosevelt was one memory that did not evaporate among his fellow Confederate veterans.

In 1912, McDowell closed out his farm and moved to Shelby County, where he spent his last fifteen years.

According to his obituary, McDowell's death represented

> *the passing of a conspicuous figure in Tennessee politics, even though his political loves were many…He contended against political forces that were merciless…He was the last of the Populist leaders, except Buchanan. The historian of the future must indeed be false to his purpose and recreant to his trust if, in the stirring life of John Hugh McDowell, he fails to find a character well worth a right sizable story.*

6

PETER TURNEY V. HENRY CLAY EVANS IN THE DISPUTED GUBERNATORIAL ELECTION OF 1894

The 1890s were a time of political unrest in the nation at large, especially when one considers the ferment generated by the nontraditional Farmers' Alliance or, as it manifested itself in Tennessee, the Farm-Labor Coalition. John Price Buchanan was the first working Tennessee farmer to be elected to the governor's post in 1890. In 1892, he ran against Democratic Party candidate Peter Turney, who won the contest.

Turney, Tennessee's twenty-eighth governor, was from Marion County and was the son of one of Tennessee's United States senators, Hopkins Turney, who had been selected by the Democrats' "Immortal Thirteen." He was educated as an attorney and by 1848 had his own practice. During the Civil War, he raised a regiment even before Tennessee seceded from the Union. He was wounded and returned to service in Florida. In his absence, his Tennessee plantation home was burned by advancing Federal soldiers. He returned to Tennessee after the war and once again took up his law practice. In 1870, he was elected to the state supreme court, where he remained as a justice until his election on the Democratic ticket in 1892. In his first term, Turney ended the prisoner-lease system and established Brushy Mountain Prison, which put prisoners to work mining coal, ending the Coal Creek War, and provided coal for the capitol, asylums and many other public buildings. He was renominated by his party for a second term in 1894.

The Republican Party, unable to win the governor's seat since 1880 with the election of Alvin Hawkins, ultimately settled on the dynamic

Portrait of Peter Turney.

Chattanoogan Henry Clay Evans as its standard bearer. According to historian and one former chairman of the Tennessee Historical Commission, Robert E. Corlew, Evans was a Pennsylvania-born entrepreneur/industrialist with extensive business interests in East Tennessee. Evans was no stranger to politics, having served four terms as a Chattanooga alderman, two terms as mayor and one term as a United States congressman.

While in Congress, he supported the Lodge Federal Election Bill, or the "Force Bill." It was designed to provide for the supervision of federal elections by the national government in order to protect African American voters in the South from state measures designed to deprive them of the vote. The "Force Bill" was a measure that was not popular among Southern whites, and it failed in the U.S. Senate. Evans's support for the failed legislation earned him the title of "Force Bill Evans" in the Democratic press, and it cost him reelection to the House in 1890 and 1892. It also worked to undermine his popularity in the election of 1894. As the Republican Party's standard bearer, he promised to make a rigorous speaking canvass of the state, and because he was regarded as a man of pleasant appearance and as an articulate and vigorous speaker, he would be able to keep his promises.

To complicate the election was the presence of the Populist Party, which was the first to choose its gubernatorial candidate, a Davidson County schoolteacher named A.L. Mimms. He was mocked by the Democrats and Republicans alike as "Professor Mimms" during the campaign. The Populists opposed the poll tax and the uniform ballot law. The Prohibitionist Party, which first ran a gubernatorial candidate in 1888, failed to nominate a candidate of its own but adopted a platform that was in agreement with the Populists and so supported that party's nominee. Members of either party realized they had little or no chance of winning the contest, but as an editorial in the *Gainesboro Gazette* stated, "A vote for Mims [*sic*] is half a vote for Evans."

Governor Turney began his reelection campaign in Middle Tennessee, at Murfreesboro, on September 13. "Old Pete" spoke briefly to the assembled just before lunch, and after an hour of rest and refreshments, he again took his place on the podium to resume his speech. The governor, however, was able to speak only for a few minutes and had to retire and let his brother finish his speech. Democrats realized that their candidate was too feeble to attract many votes, especially when compared to the compelling and dynamic speaking style of Evans. To counter the threat of certain defeat, the Democrats enlisted the aid of Edward Ward Carmack, the peppery editor of the *Memphis Commercial Appeal*, who conducted Turney's campaign from Bristol to Memphis. The governor would speak only once more—on Labor Day in a stump speech in Chattanooga.

Evans's campaign opened in Huntingdon on September 5 and ended on November 5 in Ashland City. Evans had the help of William McKinley, then Republican senator from Ohio, who spoke for him at the Cheatham County seat on the closing day of the campaign. Evans concentrated his eloquence on national politics and the follies of Democratic president Grover Cleveland's monetary policies. He criticized Turney as the "business candidate" while Turney's spokesman Carmack alleged the same of Evans. Turney, while he never actually said Evans was a "carpetbagger," did attempt to link his name with that of William G. Brownlow, the Radical Republican governor from the Reconstruction era.

The election was held on November 6, and the next day the press reported that it was without doubt the closest vote ever cast in Tennessee's history. It was generally taken for granted that the legislature was securely in the Democratic camp but that Evans had shown a remarkable increase over the 1892 vote gained by the Republican Party. "Old Pete" had lost significant support in Shelby and Davidson Counties and in other counties in Middle Tennessee.

The unofficial vote, tallied by November 10, seemed to reveal that the GOP had made gains in all of the state's counties and that Evans had been elected by a plurality of a mere 700 votes. The Turney campaign insisted, however, that once the official vote was tallied, the Democrats would be shown to have won the election. Unhappily for Governor Turney, however, the official vote showed the Democrats with 104,356 votes, the Republicans with 105,104 and the Populists with 23,088. The Evans campaign claimed victory, but the Democrats refuted that mandate, saying that in East Tennessee, long a Republican stronghold, many had cast their ballots without having first paid their poll taxes. The Turney forces claimed this also was true in Shelby and Davidson and some other Middle Tennessee counties where Evans had seemingly picked up so many votes. If true, this would mean many votes were fraudulently cast, and the apparent Republican victory would be placed in serious question. On December 12, the secretary of state announced that Evans had won the election by 748 votes. On the day after Christmas in 1894, Turney declared that he would contest the election of Evans.

By January 4, 1895, the State Democratic Executive Committee, headquartered in Nashville, had charged the Republican Party with "reckless disregard of law" in the November election and urged the heavily Democratic General Assembly to investigate the possibility of fraud, especially in regard to voting without payment of the poll tax. Nevertheless, confident in his victory, Evans set up his headquarters in the Maxwell House Hotel on the seventh, and traveled to Washington, D.C., where he made a speech saying he was certain that the Democratic legislature would "count me out" of the office.

It was not until February 5, 1895, that the two houses of the General Assembly met to canvass vote returns. Sitting on the right and representing Governor Turney were John J. Vertrees, W.H. Carroll and J.W. Gaines; on the left sat Evans and his attorneys John Ruhm Sr., G.N. Tillman and Colonel A.S. Colyar. With the speaker of the senate Ernest Pillow presiding, only sixteen of the sixty-seven counties being examined were not challenged.

In the interim, efforts were made, on February 6, to swear Evans in as Tennessee's twenty-ninth governor before the joint session of the legislature, but objections from Duncan Cooper, the Democrat floor leader for the Davidson County delegation, successfully moved for adjournment. Evans's efforts were apparently thwarted, but taking the matter in hand, he was sworn in as governor in the state library. Yet matters grew even more complicated when Secretary of State W.S. Morgan refused to record the swearing in.

Soon thereafter, Governor Turney filed with the speaker of the senate the specifications of his claim for fraudulent voting in thirty-four counties. On Valentine's Day, the General Assembly organized a "Committee of the Governor's Election" to consider and report findings on alleged voting fraud. Seven of the twelve members were Democrats, and the remaining five were Republicans. The committee was divided into three subcommittees for each of the three grand divisions to investigate the returns for sixty-three counties. By March 12, the subcommittee investigating East Tennessee returns reported that Evans had lost a total of six thousand votes in that region due to nonpayment of the poll tax. On the twenty-sixth, Cordell Hull, chairman of the Middle Tennessee committee, began looking at Davidson County returns. It was not long thereafter, on April 2, that Evans supporters who opposed the procedures used to investigate the election held a mass meeting in Nashville. The meeting was broken up by rowdies, an action the weekly publication the *Chat* called a "disgrace to the city." On the thirteenth, a meeting of Democrats in Nashville called for the legislature to halt the investigation and seat Evans without further delay.

On April 22, the General Assembly reconvened, and John J. Vertrees addressed the Hull Committee meeting in the House in support of Governor Turney. Six days later, a report was filed with the Committee of the Election of the Governor by W.P. Caldwell, committee chairman, which designated Turney the winner by a plurality of only 2,358 votes. The report was signed by the seven Democratic committee members, while the five Republicans refused to sign. The vote on May 4 was 70 to 57 to accept the committee's majority judgment, and on May 8, 1895, Peter Turney was inaugurated for his second term as governor of Tennessee.

Evans may have lost the election, but he gained notoriety as a Republican martyr and hero. He would briefly be considered as the vice-presidential running mate in 1894 and became commissioner of federal pensions under President William McKinley. In that position, he earned the enmity of the Grand Army of the Republic by eliminating some 3,500 veterans from the pension list, men he claimed were not disabled and thus not entitled to a government pension. He was thereafter appointed consul general in London by President Theodore Roosevelt. His political career ended in 1905, when he left England and returned to Chattanooga.

Turney's triumph was secured at the sacrifice of Democratic Party synergy. The party split widely between the new industrialist wing and the by-now-old neo-Confederate wing. Quite a number of Democratic papers declared that the election was in its complexity and dishonesty behind only the Tilden-Hays presidential election of 1876. Turney thus began his second term with little support from a very large portion of his own party. Dissension was caused by the administration's failure to appropriate the necessary funds for the Tennessee Centennial Exposition, high expenditures encompassed in convening the legislature for two extra sessions, the so-called Paste Pot affair in which Governor Turney's enemies charged that two of his confidants acquired $3,000 for pasting a few coupons on canceled bonds and failure to appraise railroad corporation assets at their real worth. These events brought increased dissidence in Democratic Party ranks and, as Corlew put it, "made

Portrait of Henry Clay Evans.

evident to all that Turney's administration would pass unwept, unhonored, and unsung." Turney would lose his third bid for the Democratic nomination for governor to Robert L. "Our Bob" Taylor. Turney returned to Winchester to resume his legal career, but his fragile constitution precluded any active work in the courts. He died in 1903 and was buried in Winchester.[2]

7
EDITORIAL CARTOONS V. MONOPOLY

THE *NASHVILLE DAILY AMERICAN* AGAINST THE ST. LOUIS AND NASHVILLE RAILROAD

In September 1887, the voters of Davidson County and the city of Nashville were asked to approve a bond issue aimed at building the Tennessee Midland Railroad. It promised competition with the existing Louisville and Nashville (L&N) Railroad and its nominal competitor the Nashville, Chattanooga and St. Louis Railroad, a regional monopoly. The ensuing battle over the subsidy was fought in the editorial columns in both the pro-Midland *Nashville Daily American* and the advocate for the L&N, the *Nashville Banner*. A unique characteristic of this fight was the use of the contemporary editorial cartoons by the *Daily American*.[3]

Throughout the latter part of the nineteenth century, the Louisville and Nashville Railroad gained a reputation as one of the most efficient and profitable railroads in the South, if not in the nation. Partly, this was the result of its business practices, which resulted in an absolute monopoly between its two termini and in turn allowed it to effectively engage and halter rival economic competition, the curse of monopoly. According to one author, after 1900, the L&N's tendency toward waging public, large-scale political efforts in such southern states as Alabama and Kentucky is well illustrated.[4] Yet at least once before 1900, the L&N carried out an effective campaign to thwart the development of a rival railroad, the Tennessee Midland, in 1887 in Nashville and Davidson County. It is not going too far to suggest that its actions served as a model defining action in similar efforts in the future. This was carried out in a political context in which the anti-railroad monopoly Farmers' Alliances were evolving into the nation's third-largest political organization, the Populist Party. The positive values inherent in that shift included individualism, economic freedom and competition and a strategy to link rural, urban and black workers to obtain economic justice.[5] The 1887 issue revolved around the question of whether public support should be translated into a public subscription to fund competition for the L&N. The narrative has been unnoticed in Tennessee historiography until now.

The L&N had gained its monopoly stature by the close of the 1860s. Its initial success was partly a matter of gaining public support for the road before the Civil War. It ran along what was essentially a north-to-south axis. The Midland, on the other hand, had not one mile of track laid by 1887, although it had completed its survey of what was basically an east–west route. It was breaking new ground, although the idea of such a railroad had been discussed for decades before the outbreak of war. The construction relied on public support. The actual building of the road represented a dangerous threat to the L&N—and to a lesser extent the Nashville and Chattanooga (N&C)—and could not be allowed to proceed. Moreover, the actual fight for public subscription took on clear tones of moneyed power versus the common man. The effort in Davidson County and Nashville occurred in the context of the emergence of Populism from its Farmers' Alliances antecedents, although as a political movement it had not surfaced in Tennessee until 1887.[6] In this aspect, it represented an early manifestation of the Populist strategy to tie rural with urban and black workers to obtain economic justice through the political means. Biracial political rallies and ethnic block voting during the first phases of the Jim Crow era are at odds with interpretations of the beginnings of segregationist policies.[7] The effort likewise revealed a Populist tendency toward xenophobia. Pinkerton detectives, corrupt electoral practices and bribery were publicized as weapons by the L&N to maintain its monopoly and defeat the subscription. This was ironic in that the L&N's early success was in part a result of public support. For example, Louisville and the government of Warren County, Kentucky, twice passed a referendum to purchase stock in the early history of the L&N.[8] A hostile takeover in 1880 allowed the L&N a majority interest in Nashville, Chattanooga and St. Louis stock, and the two operated virtually as separate entities, although always in each other's interest.

In August 1887, after nearly two years of effort, the Tennessee Midland Railroad Company had completed its survey for a route from Memphis to Bristol, Tennessee, with grandiose plans to stretch all the way to the Atlantic

Ocean in Norfolk, Virginia. The route would begin in Memphis, running to the point where the Virginia state line crossed the Clinch River.[9]

The fight began after backers of the Midland project gained approval to hold a referendum that would put the matter of public subscription to the voters. The *American*, a solidly Democratic Party paper, was in favor of the project, and the *Nashville Banner*, substantially Republican in orientation, was against the Midland project. It was a classic conflict between economic concentration and the ideal of competition. The *Banner*'s editor, Edward B. Stahlman, was coincidentally a third vice-president of the L&N, a fact that wasn't wasted on the editors of the *American*. Yet the *American* could not throw the first stone inasmuch as its leading officer, A.S. Colyar, was a vice-president of Tennessee Iron and Coal Company, ironically the subject of two *Banner* cartoons in 1885[10] against its practice of leasing convicts to work in the coal mines.

Portrait of A.S. Colyar.

The *American* utilized editorials, cartoon art, beer and political rallies in its campaign to persuade voters to approve the referendum. It was not shy in appealing to proto-Populist xenophobia and emasculating threats the monopoly symbolized to voters' manhood. The *Banner* likewise staged rallies while L&N company officers made threats of joblessness to L&N workers if they dared vote for the Midland subsidy. Resorting to bribery was not unknown either. More conservative editorials castigated the project as a charade. Neither did the L&N hesitate to recruit voters from along its line and hire crews of Pinkerton detectives to spy on and intimidate workers. Both sides courted the African American vote, which was robust in its appearance in the initial days of Jim Crow. It is not difficult to deduce how the battle went, but it is significant that it permanently quashed the Midland project. Monopoly triumphed over the ideal of competition. Perhaps more important, however, are the visual documents generated by the controversy, part of what can legitimately be called one of the first, if not *the* first, nineteenth-century visual media campaigns in Tennessee political and economic history. The following do not represent the full number of these cartoons but a sampling that is captivating in its focus and iconic imagery, as well as entertaining as editorial/political art. They are visual documents worthy of further research and study.

THE FIGHT IS ON

In this, the first of many cartoons published in the *Nashville Daily American* in September 1887 (see Figure 1), it is announced on the sixth that the fight for a public railroad subsidy had begun. The Midland, not yet a railroad but merely a proposal, sought public funding for its construction, which was opposed by the monopoly L&N railroad. Here, a heroic St. George figure clad in medieval armor prepares to fight the vicious, stiletto-toothed L&N dragon that holds a nearly unconscious damsel, representing "Lady Nashville," dressed in classical Grecian costume and vaguely reminiscent of the Statue of Liberty, in its sharp, scaly clutches. The plumed knight holds a sword labeled "competition" and a shield with the motto "Vox Pop." Third vice-president of the L&N and editor of the opposition newspaper, the *Nashville Banner*, Edward B. Stahlman goads the L&N dragon, symbolizing monopoly, on to combat with the knight

Figure 1.

representative of free market competition. Nashville's economy is visibly distressed by the L&N monopoly. The dragon's crest is characterized by a section of railroad ties and steel rails. The plump Stahlman's top hat is typical of the attire worn by cartoon characterizations of monopolists of the day. This cartoon, like most of those that followed up to the vote on the twenty-second, appeared on the first page of the *American*. It would have been difficult not to discern the cartoon's meaning. It was the nineteenth-century equivalent to late twentieth- and early twenty-first-century "negative advertising." The identity of the cartoonist (or cartoonists) is unknown.

L&N Railroad

The reality of the L&N monopoly's strong impounding of state government (symbolized by the capitol), economy and indeed the entire city of Nashville is represented in this cartoon appearing in the *Nashville American* of September 8, 1887 (see Figure 2). A medieval theme is again

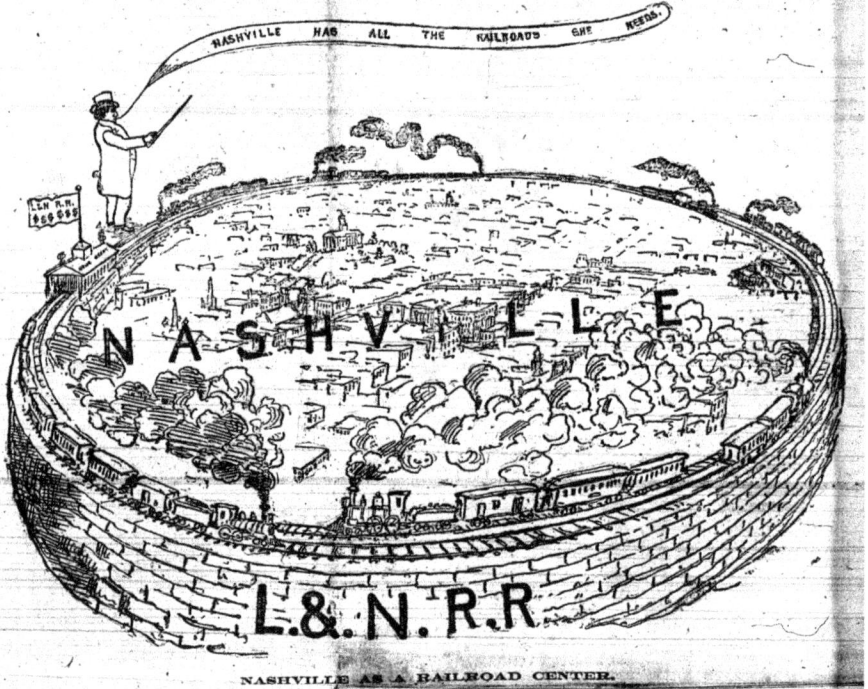

Figure 2.

utilized, that of a walled city, in which L&N trains pass in order along the fortress's ramparts as sentries, protecting the city from competition. The walled city has no facility for entrance or egress. The caption reads, "Nashville as a Railroad Center." The commanding top-hatted Stahlman is seen in the distance, standing just outside the wall, disciplinary rod in hand, declaring, "Nashville has all the railroads she needs." A flag on the L&N station (just left and below Stahlman) has as its device dollar signs underneath the letters L&N.

MONOPOLY SQUIRMS

The cartoon in the *American* for September 9, 1887, illustrated a concerted attack on the sequestered L&N bastion (see Figure 3). It was entitled "Monopoly Squirms." In the foreground leading the assault are trains from the "Tennessee Midland RR" approaching the city atop railroad trestles. Underneath the trestles are other Midland trains leaving via the arched egress, labeled the "Midland Station," penetrating the stout L&N wall. Midland railroad cars are labeled "Low Rates" and "Coal—At Better Prices," indicating the desired effect of competition. The L&N wall is labeled "High Rates, No Competition." L&N trains symbolically continue their now largely impotent anti-competition patrol atop the ramparts while a viciously screaming "monopoly" dragon with an arrowhead-tipped tongue, an image first introduced on the sixth, defends the city. A "vote bomb" soars hissing through the air at the dragon, symbolizing the explosive power of the franchise against monopoly.

Figure 3.

Figure 4.

Figure 5.

LOQUENCE AND NTERPRISE

The proto–Rube Goldberg image in the *American* cartoon of September 10, 1887 (see Figure 4), was designed to illustrate the manner in which the L&N worked to corrupt the vote on the Midland subscription ballot. To the right, on a railroad trestle, is an L&N train literally dumping large amounts of money into a funnel that reaches, to no one's surprise, the office of Edward B. Stahlman, third vice-president of the L&N. The cash is deposited in large barrels from which Stahlman ladles generous portions and pours them into yet another funnel and thus into the pockets of a wily speaker standing atop a beer barrel to the left. The speaker is addressing a largely African American audience. L&N cash is thus being employed behind the scenes to affect the black vote on the Midland issue. The clever slogans "Behind the Scenes" and "Loquence & Nterprise," reinforce the symbolic imagery of the cartoon's message.

WHAT COMPETING RAILROADS WILL DO FOR NASHVILLE

Competition meant the ruin of the L&N's grip on the city of Nashville, if the symbolism of this *American* cartoon of September 11, 1887, plus the caption "What Competing Railroads Will Do for Nashville" are interpreted correctly (see Figure 5). The destruction of the L&N's "great wall" of Nashville is represented by the devastation of the barrier, its stone blocks strewn about with abandon and railroad tracks ripped asunder. The city is compensated by the introduction of the Midland Railroad. The scene is reminiscent of the destruction of Atlanta, Georgia, in 1864. The cartoon claims Nashville supported a population of 200,000, all of whom were now set free from the demon monopoly. The banner over the L&N depot, seen to the upper left, is flying from a leaning flagstaff, as compared to the robust symbol of the healthy Midland flagpole. The Midland Railroad Station symbolizes the hearty freedom and victory over the L&N with six track lines emanating from its impressive Romanesque Revival depot, an architectural symbol of imposing strength and solidarity.

Fable of the Weeping Crocodile

The *American* cartoon of September 13, 1887, presented another symbolic reptilian representation for the L&N monopoly, that of a crocodile (see Figure 6). In fact, this particular symbol for the L&N was utilized often in the remaining nine days of the subsidy campaign. In the cartoon, captioned "The Fable of the Weeping Crocodile," a "Large and Nergectic" crocodile converses with an "Unsophisticated Citizen." The gist of the conversation reveals that a firm in Holland controlled the L&N, and consequently the

Figure 6.

"Holland Crocodile" was the new symbol for the L&N monopoly. The beast, of course, cries crocodile tears while unsuccessfully attempting to convince the "Unsophisticated Citizen" to vote against the Midland subscription. The "Holland Crocodile" is an emblematic locomotive, pulling a long tail of L&N boxcars. Symbolic appeals to American xenophobia are clear.

NASHVILLE IN THE TOILS

The "monopoly" anaconda wraps itself in a death grip around the symbol for economic freedom, the classically clad iconic "Lady Nashville" (see Figure 7). The symbolism of her similarity to the Statue of Liberty is evident. At her side is a prophylactic shield, labeled "Progress," which, in her present circumstance, is no longer of any value to her. The black serpent, "Monopoly," opens its expansive fang-contoured mouth while flicking its

Figure 7.

tongue, about to strike and keep "Nashville in the Toils." Yet help arrives in the nick of time in the form of a stalwart axe-wielding yeoman farmer whose belt is labeled "competition." He will dispatch the serpent and symbolically rescue progress from monopoly. The extended caption of this September 15, 1887 *American* cartoon reinforces the visual message that "competing lines—is all she needs to rise like a Queen among her sister cities...rise like freemen, and teach this foreign corporation that you dare stand like men in defense of your rights." Such symbolic imagery predated by only a few years the populist fight against monopoly.

IMMENSE! OMNIVOROUS!! INSATIATE!!!

The immense monster crocodile with a collar designated "Holland Crocodile" appeared in a naturally prone position in the *American*'s cartoon of September 16, 1887 (see Figure 8). Citizens ranging in occupation from urban merchants to farmers, carpenters and industrial workers bring sustenance in the form of grain and money to the wide-mouthed, leering crocodile whose tail, like that of the first appearance of the reptile on the thirteenth, is a train of L&N box cars stretching phantasmagorically into a pastoral landscape. The larger caption indicates, with increasing alarm designated by an increasing number of exclamation points, that the monster monopoly would consume all of Davidson County's and Nashville's wealth. The crocodile is gratuitously labeled "No Competition Allowed." The image also hints at the symbolic possibility that the Holland Crocodile will even consume the Nashvillian forced to feed it—such were the dangers of monopoly.

THE AMSTERDAM CYCLONE

The *American* full-front-page cartoon of September 18, 1887, was a partial salvage of the illustration of the sixteenth (see Figure 9). An even larger Holland Crocodile consortium was symbolically responsible for an immense tornado funneling horses, sheep, mules, swine, cattle, geese, goats and grain into the mouth of the "L.&N.R.R." A sign in the background identifies "Middle Tennessee Farms Without Rail Road Commission," from whence the tornado emanates. A small figure to the left, an apparent urban dweller,

IMMENSE! OMNIVOROUS!! INSATIATE!!!

Above: Figure 8. *Below*: Figure 9.

THE AMSTERDAM CYCLONE—TRUTH WITHOUT POETRY!

holds on to a torn tree trunk and exclaims, "It's about to get me too." The giant monopoly was symbolically able to harness the forces of nature to gluttonously feed itself with the livelihood of hapless farmers.

DETECTIVES RIVETING THE SHACKLES ON NASHVILLE

Perhaps one of the more compelling cartoons to appear in the *American* was that of September 19, 1887 (see Figure 10). Lady Nashville with her now useless shield of progress at her side is restricted as she is manacled by a crew of detectives. Edward B. Stahlman, this time without his top hat, holds her right arm while T.G. Hewlett, a notorious L&N detective, fastens the iron

Figure 10.

manacles on her left arm. A Pinkerton detective secures what could be called the "shackles of tyranny" around her ankles. A gang of Pinkertons hovers in the background eager to help in the work. To the right is the recently transmogrified whip-toting Holland Crocodile, who supervises the work. Here Lady Nashville, the symbolic representation of the city, is restricted so she may be controlled by the hideous half man–half crocodile monopoly fiend. The L&N would stop at little to render competition impotent. The resemblance between Lady Nashville and the Statue of Liberty is striking, particularly insofar as the foot irons, or "shackles of tyranny," are also placed on her. (The "Shackles of Tyranny" are broken at the feet of the Statue of Liberty, which was inaugurated on October 28, 1886.)

A Delectable Spectacle

During the campaign, it was reported that Edward B. Stahlman had visited L&N shops to threaten workers with discharge should they vote for the Midland subscription. In the September 17, 1887 number of the *American* (see Figure 11), a now surrealistically metamorphosed and hideous Holland Company whip-cracking crocodile is symbolically portrayed holding dismissal notices over the ballot box to coerce workers' votes. They laugh, demonstrating that their manhood and honesty are validated as they vote defiantly against their employer. "A Delectable Spectacle," read the caption. The reader is reminded by apparent graffiti in the background of the image that "This Is a Free Country." While the mustachioed workmen recognized the results of their labor belonged to the Holland Crocodile, their "manhood" was their own. One defiantly holds a ballot marked "For the Midland." They could not be intimidated and approved of competition, not monopoly. The cartoon symbolized an anticipated growing power and political awareness of the working class in Nashville.

He Dared to Assert His Freedom

While there were smaller and less dramatic cartoons published in the back pages of the *American*, the front-page drawing on the twenty-first, the eve of

Figure 11.

the Midland subscription vote, carried the bold caption "He Dared to Assert His Freedom" (see Figure 12). The perfectly dressed and whip-brandishing Holland-Crocodile is shown handing a discharge notice to Samuel S. Roche. A fifteen-year veteran of the L&N, he had been terminated because he voiced his opinion, while off the job, that he favored competition and therefore the passage of the Midland subscription. This the L&N would not tolerate, having adamantly recommended that all its employees toe the line and vote as the company dictated—otherwise the corporation would force the employee "to step down and out." Roche, with folded arms, takes a bold, manly stand, refusing to take the discharge papers while his dismayed and frowning spouse comforts the couple's frightened children. Roche was the victim of a latter-

Figure 12.

day version of "political correctness." The entire cartoon symbolized the new power of the corporation to manipulate freedom of speech and the franchise to favor its own ends, a phenomenon then relatively new in American political life.

HARD AT WORK

On election day, September 22, two *American* cartoons deserve attention. The first, captioned "Hard at Work" (see figure 13), was meant to convince the average voter that the L&N would do to any erring employees what it did

Figure 13.

to Samuel Roche. Seen at a table, visible to the viewer, are the now wholly devolved primal Holland Crocodile and "Me Too" Edward B. Stahlman. With his back to the viewer is Milton H. Smith, first vice-president of the L&N, identified by the name on the back of his chair. Both men take orders from their reptilian chief and obediently write discharge notices to all the company's employees known to have expressed their desire to vote for the Midland subscription. A railroad detective-spy, most likely T.G. Hewlett, is seen scurrying to their table with a list of disloyal employees. Workers, symbolized by brawny blacksmiths pounding their hammers at L&N shops, are seen in the background. No doubt their names were on the list being hastened to the executives' desk. The architectural symbolism of the Romanesque arches in the background suggests luxury and the atmosphere if not attitude associated with the paternalistic Latin American plantation.

THE FATE OF THE HOLLAND CROCODILE

The second cartoon to appear in the *American* on the twenty-second (see Figure 14) indicates that no matter what the L&N's economic power might be, it was not enough to overcome the American Constitution and the law. In the drawing, captioned "The Fate of the Holland Troops—A Barrier They Can't Fire Over," are seen Edward B. Stahlman, T.G. Hewlett and Milton H. Smith. "General Smith" sits astride a rearing Holland Crocodile with sword in hand. Stahlman makes the hesitant allusion to the 1885 defeat of a Tennessee Railroad Commission, saying, "This Won Before, I Am Not So Sure This Time." T.G. Hewlett unquestioningly pulls the lanyard of the massive mortar-like "corruption gun" at Smith's command, "Fire!" The cannon fires an immense charge of money and a cur dog representing the *Banner* at voters marching to the polls. The symbolic wall of "The Constitution & the Law," however, shields the great throng of determined pro-Midland voters from the heavy-handed "military and industrial complex" assaults of the L&N.

Figure 14.

How the Battle Was Won

Despite the hullabaloo raised by the cartoons in the *American*, the Midland subsidy vote was lost by the slim margin of 2 percent. The cartoon of the twenty-third (see Figure 15) was an adaptive reuse of the previous day's caricature with a new caption, "How the Battle Was Won." In it the much-revered wall of the Constitution and law proved no barrier to the blast of the corruption gun. Still astride the bucking crocodile, "General" Smith raises his sword and triumphantly exclaims, "Our Vassals Yet!" Top-hatted Edward Stahlman holds a discharge notice and an emblematic enlarged golden double eagle, saying, "We Win Again." Hewlett's part in the defeat is characterized by a better aim as he continues his artillery responsibilities, firing a hurricane of money, the dog *Banner* and a variety of detritus at Midland voters. The L&N had defeated the fearful competition of the Midland subscription and maintained control of its monopoly, as the cartoon symbolized, by use of newspaper editorials, tricks, money and lies.

Figure 15.

ELECTION RESULTS

Election results were published in the September 23, 1887 *Daily American*.

NASHVILLE VOTE TALLY BY WARD

	PRO-MIDLAND	ANTI-MIDLAND
First Ward	257	42
Second Ward	563	98
Third Ward	815	102
Fourth Ward	540	106
Fifth Ward	475	108
Sixth Ward	727	246
Seventh Ward	712	277
Eighth Ward	573	299
Ninth Ward	527	417
Tenth Ward	416	315
Eleventh Ward	655	71
Twelfth Ward	231	112
Thirteenth Ward	231	252+
Fourteenth Ward	298	80
Total	7,230	2,223

DAVIDSON COUNTY VOTE TALLY BY DISTRICT AND PRECINCT

	Pro-Midland	Anti-Midland
Second District		
First Precinct	156	84
Second Precinct	165	85
Third District	*	*
Fourth District	90	129+
Fifth District	113	68
Sixth District	206	6

	Pro-Midland	Anti-Midland
Seventh District	*	*
Eighth District	87	139+
Ninth District	312	56
Tenth District	633	223
Eleventh District	138	82
Twelfth District		
First Precinct	614	294
Second Precinct	865	392
Fourteenth District	90	128+
Fifteenth District	216	71
Sixteenth District	*	*
Seventeenth District	200	73
Eighteenth District	320	40
Nineteenth District	90	91+
Twentieth District	113	179+
Twenty-first District	106	22
Twenty-second District	*	*
Twenty-third District	137	322+
Twenty-fourth District	*	*
Twenty-fifth District	*	*
Total	4,741	2,224
Total Wards	7,280	2,223
Grand Total	11,971	4,417

Nashville/Davidson County Midland Subscription Vote Tally.
* There is no explanation given for the missing tallies from these districts.
+ Indicates anti-Midland majority

SOMETHING FOR GOOD CITIZENS TO
THINK ABOUT

The last cartoon on the subject of the Midland subsidy appeared in the *American* on September 25, 1887 (see Figure 16). In it, a sandaled Miss Nashville, yet again symbolized as a caricature of the Statue of Liberty,

Figure 16.

holds the odiferous "Holland Crocodile" at arm's length, unrolling a scroll asking if the gateway of prosperity had been closed by the L&N "And This Monster Keep the Key?" The sneering cartel L&N crocodile, keeping the key to prosperity tucked tightly in its monopoly belt, displays its own scroll with the tauntingly direct exclamation, "Well, what are you going to do about it?" The caption admonished, "Something for Good Citizens to Think About." As it turned out, nothing was or could be done. Nashville and the nation at large were entering a new economic era and a new phase of social development.[11] Concentration now held sway over customary economic and political freedom. There was no turning back, symbolically or otherwise.

8

THE ANTI-SUFFRAGE CRUSADE IN TENNESSEE, 1912–1920

The year 2015 marks the ninety-fifth anniversary of the final campaign to guarantee female suffrage in the United States of America. Tennessee women were dominant in the fight to add the Nineteenth Amendment to the U.S. Constitution in 1920. Already the U.S. Congress and thirty-five states had ratified the amendment, but still one more state was needed to add it to the Constitution. Tennessee became the pivotal state in the long battle for women's suffrage. The very topic of equal rights for women challenged the fundamental principle of domestic belief that rested securely on the concept of the separation of male and female spheres and the mediocrity of women. While there was overwhelming women's support for the notion of equality between the sexes in Tennessee, there was also a vocal minority of Tennessee women who, experiencing class and status anxiety, opposed equality between the spheres and worked to defeat the amendment. They feared not only that their status in society would be eroded but also, and even worse, that others they considered beneath them would soon rule. They earnestly believed that if women got the vote it would destroy the very foundations of civilization. That this status quo crusade ultimately did not prevail is less important than is the fact that it symbolized a backward-looking passion to maintain the old Victorian concept of two spheres, the outside world being the province of the predatory male, and the inside, or domestic and culture-nurturing world, being the separate sphere of the other sex. In short, it was the lost cause for the "antis," the self-proclaimed champions of domestic values and a separate women's sphere for which they unyieldingly struggled.

At first, the anti-suffrage campaign was unorganized in Tennessee. There was little need to organize from 1900 to 1912 because there was really little threat of women's suffrage becoming a reality. The spheres would remain separate. But as the suffragist movement gained ground in Tennessee and the state became tactically important in the crusade, opposition would consolidate, adopting the red rose as its symbol.

Manifestations of opposition to the suffragist movement before 1912 are found in letters to newspapers. In one exemplary letter to the *Nashville Banner* on October 12, 1912, a Mrs. L.H. Hicks wrote that men had a divine right to rule the entire world. She used a biblical basis for her conjecture, that God had always had the governing power from the outset and that Christ had sanctioned the existing order. Her feelings on the matter were best justified in her estimation because "men have made the earth a beautiful protected home for the human race, especially the women." Women could never be the equals of men because it was "ordained from the first that man should be in control...and hysterical argument cannot put them aside." Therefore, ran this gender-based and self-hate diatribe, women should not have the right to vote, she continued, because among other reasons:

> [Women] *are not logical. Women have not the power of great concentration. They easily tire...They are not mathematicians...They are impatient of just criticisms and their methods are devious, complicated and hard to follow...We have yet to produce a woman of the first caliber* [sic], *great as men are great.*

M.P. Murphy of Columbia, in a letter to the *Nashville Tennessean* of March 9, 1914, also believed that divine precepts forbade women from participating in arguments "pertaining to prominence of leadership in the church of God, and human government...women should shrink from assuming a...position in government matters which...would subject them to adverse influences." History had demonstrated, claimed another correspondent to the *Tennessean*, that even when women were presented with opportunities to distinguish themselves, they had failed. It was, however, in the "more important sphere of the home, the training of the child, [that] they admit their inability by their demands for laws to help them."

According to the Minutes of the Executive Committee Meeting of the Tennessee Equal Suffrage Association in Memphis in May 1914, some women were against women's suffrage because it had long been associated in the popular mind with the abolition of slavery and free love.

Enfranchising women would have destructive results for the domestic sphere, double the electorate and thereby increase the cost of elections. Voting was men's work, mothering was a woman's proper calling and the two spheres should ever remain separate but hardly equal.

Antagonism to the notion of the extension of the vote was likewise expressed from the pulpit. The pastor of the Immanuel Baptist Church in Nashville, Dr. Rufus W. Weaver, for example, did not favor extending the franchise. This was because America did not require "more votes but better votes and the need of women was not for more freedom, but more of the bondage of love." Even though the Bible didn't expressly teach that women weren't to vote, he said, it did explain why women were to be subordinate to men. The Reverend T.H. Harrison of the Adams Presbyterian Church in Nashville addressed the topic at a revival in late October 1914. Reverend Harrison was of the opinion that the

> question of woman suffrage…is simply a key that's going to unlock the gates of hell and turn the demons loose upon the human family…women…[were] made for man's glory—to mother man…let's not give her the ballot box, but give her a home and a Bible and a child to raise and she'll make a civilization that heaven will smile on and hell [will] be appalled. The Bible makes woman a queen on the throne of the home.

Parallels to twenty-first-century fundamentalist Christian thinking are striking.

Providing a less biblical sanction, however, was one pamphlet published in Nashville by A.A. Lyon. It foresaw severely dire consequences should women be enfranchised. Families would disintegrate, and divorces would soar to new heights. Moreover, Lyon argued, since women ruled indirectly, through their roles as mothers and wives in the domestic sphere, direct power would be an offense against divine law because the Almighty had created man first and woman second. He finished by using the southern race dilemma as an argument against women's suffrage, suggesting that to enfranchise white women meant also to enfranchise black women. Lyon encouraged Tennessee's white women to "stand by the traditions of their mothers, and continue to bear aloft the spotless white banner that symbolizes the purity and chastity and the modesty that has hitherto ever been so luminously exemplified by the women of the South." Here was a direct statement of status anxiety, the fear felt by declining social elites as their status was being eroded by newly rising voters who were replacing them in a new social order.

The "antis" continued in a relatively unorganized fashion to oppose the suffrage movement until it became apparent to them that the suffragist movement in Tennessee was gaining a profound momentum of its own. As the ranks of the suffragist movement swelled, status-anxious women opposed to the notion of equal rights for their gender were compelled to organize. What may be surprising by today's standards is that the "antis" were composed of women who objected to their sex's receiving the vote under any circumstance.

As a result of a public debate on women's suffrage held in Knoxville in 1913 between Lizzie Crozier French (pro) and Annie Riley Hale (con) of Rogersville, an initial call for the formation of an anti-suffrage organization was generated. A meeting was held, but it was not until April 1916 that the Tennessee anti-suffragists could form an organization. That year, Mrs. Arthur M. Dodge of New York, president of the National Association Opposed to Woman Suffrage, was invited to Nashville by a number of "leading women of Nashville." In a speech to the women of Nashville, she said that female suffrage would neither purify politics nor accomplish what men failed to achieve by voting. According to Mrs. Dodge:

> *Woman's true progress has been made without the vote; and the women who have achieved most in the world's work, whether suffragists or anti-suffragists, have accomplished their ends where they were out of politics…it would be the direct and irrevocable loss to women if their present position was sacrificed to suffrage, with its resultant division of women into political factions.*

It was but a few days after Mrs. Dodge's speech that the Tennessee Chapter of the National Association Opposed to Woman Suffrage (TCNAOWS) took form in the home of Mrs. John J. Vertrees. Attended by forty-four of Tennessee's most socially elite women, this meeting held the uncontested opinion that "the woman's moral influence in public affairs was greater out of politics, and that doubling the electorate could confer no benefit."

At the next meeting of TCNAOWS on May 3, 1916, it selected topics for future debate that clearly indicated its apprehensions about equality. Topics included "Feminism and Socialism," "Woman's Suffrage, a Menace to Social Reform," "Women Will Not Gain by Suffrage" and "Suffrage, Not a Natural Right." At the May 16 meeting, with the ranks swollen to over two hundred, the members discussed the legal status of married women and the racist notion that women's suffrage would be dangerous in the South because it would mean the enfranchisement of African American women as well. The idea of black women being equal to white women, let alone white men, via the ballot was just more than these status-anxious, bigoted women could abide.

Reports of TCNAOWS meetings disappeared from the press after 1916, most likely a result of uncertainty generated by the debate about the American entry into the world war. That year, Mrs. Ventrees resigned her chairmanship and was succeeded by Miss Josephine A. Pearson of Monteagle.

Pearson's family lineage extended to the colonial era, and she was no stranger to public affairs, being both a southern writer and educator and serving as associate head of a number of women's colleges in Tennessee, South Carolina and Missouri. She was also a leader in the movement for the improvement of arterial roads in America and was especially active in the Dixie Highway Association, serving as its president from 1917 to 1920. Active in the American Red Cross during the war, Pearson became the guiding light of the anti-suffragist cause in Tennessee. TCNAOWS remained relatively inactive for the duration of the war, preserving its organization until 1919, to fight the ratification campaign for the Nineteenth Amendment—an event Pearson later termed "the Verdun of 1920."

While the issue was dormant, it was not unremembered, and some expressions of anti-suffragist feeling were monitored. L.D. Hill of Sparta predicted in January 1917 that the equal suffrage amendment would "bring about the destruction of civilization and social fabric which the Anglo-Saxon people have been more than a thousand years in building." The *McMinnville Southern Standard* declared in September 1918, "When we contemplate the social and political storms that are going to burst in cyclonic fury upon this country when all these pretty girls get to voting and mixing up in politics, we rather rejoice that life is short and that we haven't many more years to tarry here."

Nashville attorney John J. Vertrees, husband of the first president of TCNAOWS, wrote an effective propaganda pamphlet entitled *An Address to the Men of Tennessee on Female Suffrage.* He was decidedly antagonistic toward women's suffrage and believed participation in government was based on the power of coercion and only those who could "bear arms should have a voice in deciding questions which may lead to war, or in enacting laws which require soldiers, sheriffs, posses and policemen for their enforcement."

Moreover, he earnestly believed that because women's lives were ones "of frequent and regular periods marked by mental and nervous irritability, when sometimes even her mental equilibrium is disturbed," they should not have the vote. Vertrees also brought up the race question, showing how Miss Helen Keller, an ardent suffragette, in a letter to the National Association for the Advancement of Colored People had "urged all to advance gladly towards our common heritage…undivided by race or color or creed." In this manner, he continued to use the race issue as a tool to divide the women's suffrage movement by associating it with racial equality. Numerous other pamphlets and cartoons were circulated, all with the general message that giving the vote to women would undermine the American home and family. (See cartoons in Chapter 10.) The "antis" also expressed their philosophy in bold upper case letters in their publication *The Anti-Suffrage Ideal*:

> *THE IDEAL OF THE ANTI-SUFFRAGISTS IS THE ULTIMATE UNION OF WOMEN OF ALL CLASSES AND CREEDS ALONG NON-PARTISAN LINES, SO THAT THE INTEREST OF WOMANHOOD, CHILDHOOD AND CIVILIZATION MAY BE ADVANCED FREE FROM THE STRIFE AND DIVISION OF POLITICS, FACTIONS, AND PARTIES; AND THAT THE FUNDAMENTAL PRINCIPLES OF PATRIOTISM, MORALITY AND AMERICANISM UPON WHICH ALL GOOD CITIZENS ARE AGREED MAY BE ESTABLISHED IN THE PRESENT AND FUTURE GENERATIONS.*

Perhaps a more meaningful glimpse into the motivations of the "antis" can be found in a photograph of Miss Pearson—the grandniece of that bastion of southern rights John C. Calhoun—and Mrs. James S. Pierce Lord, president of the Southern Woman's League for the Rejection of the Susan B. Anthony Amendment, with an unidentified Tennessee Confederate Veteran taken in August 1920. In it are seen the Anti-Ratification Headquarters sign and American flags. Mrs. Lord drapes herself in a Confederate battle flag held by the revered Confederate veteran, supported in his dotage by a cane and Pearson. The portraits of Andrew and Rachel Jackson flank the trio. A handwritten caption reads in part: "Truth crushed to the Earth will rise again." Yet another indication of their anxieties was expressed in a form letter sent to TCNAOWS members. Dated August 9, 1920, it held that the suffrage movement "carries with it more than white woman's suffrage. Linking with it were three deadly principles: 1st surrender of state sovereignty; 2nd Negro Woman Suffrage; 3rd Race Equality." Here the anti-suffragists revealed most clearly their status apprehensions, their innermost fears and the motives for their atavistic crusade.

"Truth crushed to the Earth will rise again."

The really meaningful fight, however, was still ahead. Tennessee governor Albert H. Roberts convened a special session of the General Assembly in August 1920 to deal with the question of the suffrage amendment. Pro-suffragists ("suffs") and anti-suffragists arrived at the Hermitage Hotel in Nashville to lobby legislators for their positions. Miss Pearson and TCNAOWS members wore their symbolic red rose as opposed to the "suffs'" yellow rose. In this second Tennessee War of the Roses, the fight went badly for the vermilion roses on the first vote in the Senate on the thirteenth. Five days later, the House voted to reconsider its earlier negative vote.

Pearson was ensconced on the seventh floor of the Hermitage Hotel with private telephone connections, where, she confided in a reminiscence, "I locked myself, for a spell, in Room 718." It appeared quite certain that her cause was headed for defeat when she became aware that the thirty-eight anti legislators had gathered in the Hermitage Hotel lobby in the early morning. All wore red roses, and all were spirited away to Union Station to take a 3:00 a.m. train to Alabama in order to deprive the House of a working quorum. "This Red Rose Brigade," Miss Pearson wrote, "stayed in Alabama for three weeks" sustained partly by "all kinds of nice things" sent to them by the "antis" in Nashville. The effort, while dramatic, would not prevent the ratification of the Nineteenth Amendment. The legislature reconvened on August 21, and by the twenty-fourth, Governor Albert H. Roberts had signed the bill ratifying women's suffrage in the United States.

In her assessment of the failure of the "antis" to stop the amendment, Pearson believed that "the compromised vote of the 19th Amendment was ratified by political corruption and, generally believed, bribery…[it] will always be shrouded in doubt and uncertainty of some one or more of a man's dishonor!" Roberts she called "The Perfidious Governor of Tennessee!" while the legislature itself had forgotten "their oaths…to support the State Constitution! Shame thrice shame."

Interestingly Pearson, despite the contempt for the legislators, maintained her position on women's suffrage and related the following about the national election of 1920, the first in which all American women were to vote:

> On the morning of the Election of 1920—I went…to post at The Polls at Monteagle…excitement ran high! Then the Patrion [sic] of all Monteagle elections from the past…nervous, trembling came up to me—saying: "You aint agoing to vote is you—you fit it too long and too hard! Tell us what you want voted and we'll vote for you!" I did so, always I have let this long loyal friend of my late father…direct The Men of Grundy county to vote.

Thus, she surrendered her vote to another.

After pursuing a career as an educator at numerous conservative women's colleges in the South, Pearson died during World War II on November 3, 1944, twenty-four years after the ratification of the Nineteenth Amendment. Her story and the female efforts to resist the suffrage amendment that would ultimately benefit her sex are not just an idiosyncratic narrative but illustrative of the many contrasts and conflicts brought about by the forces of modernization and status anxiety in Tennessee's rich and variegated historical experience. It tells us that there was conflict in our past, real class struggle that has all too often been ignored by historians in an effort to present a history that is dominated by consensus and the notion that the only struggle in America and Tennessee was the Civil War.

9

TENNESSEE'S FIRST FEMALE CANDIDATE FOR GOVERNOR

MRS. KATE BRADFORD STOCKTON AND THE GUBERNATORIAL ELECTION OF 1936

In the national election of 1936, the Democratic and Republican Parties had competition in the form of the candidates fielded by the Socialist Labor Party, the Prohibition Party and the Socialist Party. In Tennessee's gubernatorial race that year, the Democrats nominated Congressman Gordon Browning of Huntingdon while the Republican standard-bearer was Burgin E. Dossett, superintendent of Campbell County schools. Dossett promised to end the state's prohibition laws while Browning called for a "cleanup" of "corrupt" state government and the initiation of various fiscal reforms. While Browning would win the election by a landslide, one candidate's race for the state's highest elective office would go largely unchronicled, namely that of an Allardt, Tennessee housewife who ran on the Socialist Party ticket, Mrs. Kate Bradford Stockton.

There were but a few hundred members of the Socialist Party in Tennessee in 1936, although the party had a presence in the state since 1905. Kate Bradford Stockton was one of these few visionary-idealists. She was born in California in 1880 and went with her father and mother to the Clarkrange Community in Fentress County, Tennessee, in 1884.

Although Clarkrange had meager educational facilities, it did have a very able teacher, Perry Little. His subscription school was patronized by many local families, including that of Ben Stockton. It was at this remote school that Kate Bradford met her future husband, Joseph Kelly Stockton.

According to an unpublished paper written by Tennessee Technological University history student Rebecca Vial, Kate earned her Peabody Normal

Portrait of Kate Bradford Stockton.

teaching certificate at Livingston's Old Monroe Academy, and she continued teaching at her home after her marriage. The Stocktons lived in the Stockton community in Fentress County, where his family had extensive timber holdings. By 1916, they had a family of four daughters. Joseph was elected justice of the peace and had voted for the Socialist candidate Eugene V. Debs in the national election of 1920. He continued to support the Socialist Party during the Great Depression and no doubt was a prominent factor in Kate's conversion to the Socialist cause. According to an article in the April 9, 1936 *Knoxville News-Sentinel*, Kate indicated her transformation to Socialism, largely as a result of having read Henry George's novel *Progress and Poverty* (1879). Briefly, George contended that land was a free gift of nature, that all men have equivalent rights to use the land and that it is inherently inequitable for a few to acquire great wealth by holding land that increases in worth. According to an article in the *Chattanooga Free Press* for July 23, 1936, Mrs. Stockton "and her husband have been Socialists since 1912. Motherly and very talkative, Mrs. Stockton hasn't the slightest appearance of a radical, until she begins talking." She was described by one observer as looking like

> *one's Aunt Jennie, come in from the farm for the day to sell her butter and eggs. Her mild blue eyes, her skin tanned by many summers' work in the garden, her strong capable brown hands, her neat dress with a bit of tatting at the neck—all these things summon up a picture of a woman singing while she churns, reading the Sunday School lesson before the fire.*

Opponents of her political beliefs could hardly hurl the epithet "foreigner" at Kate, for her ancestry was genuinely American. As *Nashville Tennessean* reporter Helen Dahnke wrote during the campaign:

Even the conservative Daughters of the American Revolution could not find a foreign blotch on her escutcheon. For William Bradford, who came over on the Mayflower *in 1620 and who was the first governor of a colony ever elected in America, was one of her remote grandfathers. Mrs. Stockton takes no special pride, she only holds it up to upset the prevalent idea that being a Socialist means that she is a foreigner or dangerous. Her grandfather Bradford, a graduate of Princeton College, became a Presbyterian minister and went into the wilds of Pennsylvania to preach. There in the mist* [sic] *of the mining district her father, Arthur Bradford, grew up in the steel and iron trade and from there came to Tennessee's Upper Cumberland as a farm agent and purchaser of timber and mining lands...On her mother's side Mrs. Stockton is a Scotch Robertson of the same clan which once contributed leaders to the founding of Nashville... "Having a distinguished ancestor is only good for making us see that we do not degenerate. As we country people say, it may serve to hold us up in the collar," she says with twinkling eyes.*

Another newspaper report mentioned that another of her ancestors was Richard Stockton, a signer of the Declaration of Independence. The remains of the log structure to which the Stockton family moved in 1884 are extant today near Highway 62 in the Clarkrange Community, while the Stockton House was located on what is today Highway 127 near the corner of the present intersection of Highway 62 West and Highway 127 South.

Mrs. Stockton continued to sew and cook even as a candidate for governor, although she did much prefer campaigning. She helped her husband in running their farm, and while she didn't intend to cease canvassing soon, she did plan to return home in time to can her tomatoes, "campaign or no campaign."

Mrs. Stockton described her family as "real dirt farmers. We have 500 acres which were left to my husband by his father and about 1,200 other acres acquired by purchase or by assuming other people's obligations." Kate was no stranger to work, living, as she said over fifty years ago, "in a house with no electricity. Eight or ten times a day when I am at home I carry milk to the spring-house, bringing a bucket of water with me when I return. We have an eight hour day only [when] there are eight hours before dinner and eight hours afterward. Last year I escaped the slavery of a washboard when my daughter bought a gasoline washer." Believing that because "[f]our years of Roosevelt, four years of the New Deal, four years of patches and props have failed...[and that] Big Business and the Republican Party have furnished no program to lead us out of the depression," the Socialist Party could "attain its ends by orderly methods and…upon education of the masses… to build…a better social order and a higher civilization based on production for use and not for profit."

The State Platform of the Socialist Party of Tennessee for 1936 spelled out those ends in eighteen planks: (1) reform of state government; (2) elimination of the poll tax; (3) complete freedom of speech; (4) adequate relief provisions for the unemployed; (5) the immediate end of child labor; (6) the establishment of farmers' markets to aid the farmer in selling directly to consumers: (7) the formation of a system of state-aided, cooperatively owned farms for sub-marginal or landless farmers (much like the Cumberland Homesteads' Project in Cumberland County); (8) public electrification of rural areas; (9) enforcement of the civil service law for all non-policy-forming administrative state employees; (10) more pay for the state's teachers, remunerated for by taxes on large incomes or capital; (11) the passage of laws granting the right to organize, strike and picket "without intervention by thugs, police, injunctions, or the military"; (12) economic, political and civil equality for Negroes as United States citizens; (13) total abatement by the state of back taxes owed by small home owners, while those who lost their homes since the onset of the Great Depression in 1929 would be reimbursed; (14) all homes under a valuation of $20,000 were to be exempt from taxation; (15) free use of all schoolhouses and courthouses for orderly public gatherings; (16) free textbooks for schoolchildren; (17) workers' compensations and old age pensions; and (18) passage of a Workers' Rights Amendment to the U.S. Constitution. The cover of the Socialist Platform bore a picture of Kate Bradford Stockton with the captions "Crops rot… Machines Lie Idle—Why must humans suffer? End Poverty! Vote Socialist!"

Mrs. Stockton was also interested in the emerging fight against German and Italian Fascism and, typical of Socialists and many idealists of the time, "pictured Russia as a Utopia with no unemployment and where everyone was well fed and clothed by the government. She seemed a bit stunned," according to one contemporary newspaper article, "by the suggestion that conditions in Russia were reported to be very uncomfortable. She dismissed it quickly, however, classing it with one gesture as 'propaganda.'"

In addition to being a Socialist, a gubernatorial candidate, a teacher, a mother, a homemaker, an Irish potato farmer and an avocational astronomer, Stockton was likewise a poet. One poem, written during the 1935 Nye investigation on munitions production and profiteering during World War I, was addressed to J. Pierpont Morgan, a witness before the committee. The plutocratic financier had then offered his view that women who kept no servants had so little leisure that they could not pass on any culture to their children and that he thought such women "uncivilized." The first stanza of her poem, which grew from reflection on that comment, follows:

J. Pierpont Morgan spoke his mind unthoughted [sic],
Calling the mothers who work uncivilized
He's sure that such folk must be without culture
But Morgan's sort might be surprised
To find how solitude and self-denial
And toil develops natures that are strong
Who can reach mental heights in spite of hardship
And battle disappointment with a song.

When I remember how my little mother
In spite of hardship and of toilsome hours
Still found time to read books to us and poems—
Immortal books—and of her love for flowers—
Of how she taught us ever to love beauty
And still more in love, courage, right and truth.
Respect for work and justice for all workers
When I think back on those days of my youth

It makes my blood boil when smug Pierpont Morgan
Spits on such women as "uncivilized,"
How soon we could demolish the power of Morgans
And their sort if we were just organized.
No more they'd rob us and then brag about it,
And carry out their fiendish plots of war,
If we'd unite and vote for our own interests,
A Worker's Party, knowing well what for.

She believed she was chosen as the Socialist candidate because she was a farmer and that "a woman running for governor would be a curiosity in this state, and because we farmers are independent and can speak our minds without fear of losing our jobs...It's the most un-American thing—this fear most of us have of speaking out on our convictions. This craven fear of losing our jobs is terrible." She believed that the "top-heavy profit system which benefits a few is all wrong. It is so un-American." Kate's views were those of a woman clearly ahead of, as well as out-of-step with, her time.

The campaign for governor was not haphazard. Kate alternated weeks on the trail with Herbert Harris, the national Socialist Party organizer. The crusade was to cost about $200 a month, much of which was used to keep Harris's red sound truck rolling across the state and to print campaign literature. One highway sign cleverly imitated the "Burma Shave" format, for example: "Of the Horse/and buggy we are rid/Don't vote the way/your grand-dad did/VOTE SOCIALIST!"

Her campaign took her to all major cities in Tennessee. She explained the socialist view of the distribution of wealth to female voters with a piece of yellow ribbon, dividing it into three sections, in which the longest section, representing the holdings of the rich, was three times as long as the remaining two. She returned in July to her Allardt home for a week to can vegetables, while the national Socialist candidate campaigned in her place. The red sound truck was utilized extensively in lieu of her campaigning.

Kate Bradford Stockton's indispensable miracle did not materialize in 1936, and the Democrat Gordon Browning won, receiving 332,522 votes to Republican Burgin E. Dossett's 78,292 while Kate Bradford Stockton won 3,786, or about 1 percent of the total vote cast. Her strongest draws were in Knox, Davidson, Washington and Shelby Counties. She received 118 votes in her native Fentress County, or nearly 3 percent of the total there.

After the election, Kate continued to teach and wrote a book of poems. According to Rebecca Vial, during World War II, the family moved to California. After the war, the Stocktons moved to Washington, D.C., until the late 1960s, when they returned to Fentress County. Kate and Joseph lived in a public housing development in Jamestown until 1967, when he died. Kate Stockton moved to a nursing home and continued writing children's stories, poems and short stories. She died on August 19, 1969, and her remains were placed in one of the roofed grave houses of their ancestors in the Stockton Cemetery in Fentress County. She remains the only woman in Tennessee's history to run for governor, and the story of her life provides insight into the variety of experiences in our past that gives the Volunteer State such a rich and colorful heritage.

10

AN INTRODUCTION TO THE EDITORIAL ART OF JAMES PINCKNEY ALLEY

THE FIRST CARTOONIST FOR THE MEMPHIS COMMERCIAL APPEAL

James Pinckney Alley (1885–1934) was a product of the New South. He was born in Benton, Arkansas, on January 11, 1885, the son of Reverend John Pinckney, a Methodist minister, and Melinda Everett Alley. He received what education was available from the public school system of Benton. As a boy, he was not noted as a formalist or intellectual. At an early age, Alley demonstrated his talent in sketching artwork. In school, he was frequently scolded for clandestinely drawing characterizations and artistic pictures on schoolbook flyleaves and back covers.

Once he left high school, he was apprenticed as a potter. Searching for an outlet for his creative drive, he was said to have drawn pictures on "otherwise chaste vases when the potter wasn't looking." Even so, he occasionally managed to set a pot correctly. It was soon evident that the potter's wheel was not Alley's medium of expression. In his late teens, he left Benton and headed for Little Rock, Arkansas. There he convinced the owner of an engraving shop to indulge his interest in cartooning. It was in Little Rock that Alley sold his first cartoon and so launched his professional career. That cartoon's content is unknown and is not believed to be extant.

In the 1910s, Alley reached Memphis and continued working as an artisan for the Bluff City Engraving Company. In Memphis, he found camaraderie in the city's relatively small colony of fellow engravers and commercial artists.

In 1915, Memphis underwent a particularly virulent political campaign in which the *Commercial Appeal* opposed Edward H. Crump's machine. The Bluff City Engraving Company was called on to produce an occasional cartoon,

Portrait of James Pinckney Alley, April 17, 1934.

and Alley seized an opportunity to realize his ambition to become a cartoonist. His work as a commercial cartoon artist was soon recognized by C.P.J. Mooney, publisher of the *Commercial Appeal*, and on October 31, 1915, Alley, as an independent artist, sold his first cartoon to Mooney. He sold many more in the subsequent campaign year, and his employers demanded that he choose between commercial and editorial art. The newspaper hired him in early 1916, and for the next seventeen years he produced thousands of editorial cartoons.

His first cartoons were acerbic condemnations of the Crump machine, in which he demonstrated an evident talent in producing graphic and well-proportioned editorial lampoons and comments. Within a year, America was in the European War. The war period proved to be a time of artistic development for the cartoonist. He grasped the magnitude of the war, and through his editorial art he demonstrated its tragedies, as well as American patriotism and idealism.[12]

From that point until his death, Alley's work[13] reflected a variety of concerns, including national and local elections, preparedness, the patriotism of World War I, the ascendancy of the Republican Party in the 1920s, the Mexican and Nicaraguan revolutions, disarmament treaties and other international issues. He also spotlighted public issues such as the Red Scare, the rise of the Ku Klux Klan, declining public morals, the Florida land boom, Tea Pot Dome, the GOP, pornography, evangelical religion, evolution, prohibition, the Great Depression and FDR.[14] Alley's cartoons concerning the rise of the Ku Klux Klan demonstrated his deep commitment to racial tolerance and liberalism in an otherwise intolerant nation. The Klan series was of great importance in the *Commercial Appeal*'s winning the Pulitzer Prize in journalism for meritorious service, which Alley shared with his editor Mooney in 1923. A lifelong Democrat, he took pains to lampoon the Republican Party. One of his cartoons during the election of 1924 won him national acclaim when the Democratic national committee sent hundreds of copies throughout the country. It has been judged by some as the "most colorful cartoon of the 1924 campaign."[15] His work is similar in its graphic quality and symbolic representation to the editorial art of Thomas Nast, although perhaps not so refined in its linear quality. It is nevertheless unique and of great merit.

Alley died on April 17, 1934, in Memphis of Hodgkin's disease. His son Cal took his place at the newspaper. While his son's work has been the subject of a fascinating study[16] by Charles Crawford, there has been little or no attention given to his father's work, possibly because it is known to exist only in microfilm rolls of the *Commercial Appeal*. Nevertheless, his work has both artistic and historical significance and can only help familiarize historians and students of history with an endlessly fascinating depiction of national and regional life during Alley's tenure with the *Commercial Appeal*. "He was recognized as one of America's great cartoonists," said an editorial at the time of his death. "To love him was to love truth, honor, courage and loyalty." It is time to recognize James Pinckney Alley as one of the overlooked yet truly worthy personalities in the history of Memphis and Tennessee.

His cartoons speak louder than words, but only a few of his caricatures can be presented in an effort to promote awareness and an appreciation for the work of this Memphis artist. Their pedagogical utilizations are evident, and teachers might well find them a successful medium with which to address and visually reinforce lessons in early twentieth-century history. The images presented are taken from microfilm, which accounts for the scratched appearance. These deal with the Crump political machine, women's suffrage, the Ku Klux Klan, World War I, the Tea Pot Dome scandal, the Scopes Monkey Trial, the women's suffrage Nineteenth Amendment and the "Red Scare."

AT THE BOYS' OWN BARBECUE

One of Alley's early efforts depicts the machinations of the Crump political machine in the municipal election of 1916 (see Figure 17). Future efforts were not so intricate as his early work.

Above: Figure 17. Commercial Appeal, *July 24, 1916.*

Left: Figure 18. Commercial Appeal, *November 17, 1917.*

BIDS FOR RECOGNITION

During World War I, women filled the jobs in factories left open by men for the production of war material. Alley's comment on women's suffrage (see Figure 18) illustrates a certain negative view of portly, matronly and militant suffragist pickets as opposed to the apolitical, lithesome, young women war workers whose only purpose was to help in the great struggle for civilization and democracy.

HE'S AN OLD FLIRT AFTER ALL

Alley shows here (see Figure 19) that the General Assembly was largely in favor of the Nineteenth Amendment; the legislature is posed as an elderly gentleman whose fancy is caught by a pretty young suffragette.

Figure 19. Commercial Appeal, *August 12, 1920.*

The Female Vote

The female vote became a question of immense importance during the election of 1920 after the Tennessee General Assembly approved the Nineteenth Amendment to the Constitution giving women the right to vote. Here (see Figure 20) Alley reflects the uncertainty yet acknowledges the potential and overpowering possibility of that vote.

What Is It Anyway?

In this hilarious lampoon of the Republican Party's attempt to win the female vote in the election of 1920 (see Figure 21), Warren G. Harding is presented in drag to an audience of skeptical female voters. In the end, however, Harding won by a landslide.

Fact or Fancy?

In this cartoon (see Figure 22), Alley points out the power of the Victorian image that romantically defined women as the precious image and embodiment of beauty and grace—until, that is, she wanted to vote. The male figure resents the request and hypocritically tells her to get back to the business of keeping a house and raising children.

The Two Ballot Boxes

Alley, a good Wilsonian Democrat, looked to a future in which war would be outlawed. He apparently hoped the female vote would result in the right choice of the Democrat, James M. Cox of Ohio. His use of representations of classical figures such as Mars (war) and Athena (peace) labeled "League of Nations" is typical of his work (see Figure 23). Indeed, the female form is utilized to depict not only civilization but also that the very future of civilization might well depend on the female vote.

Figure 20. Commercial Appeal, *October 14, 1920.*

Figure 21. Commercial Appeal, *October 20, 1920.*

Figure 22. Commercial Appeal, *August 14, 1920.*

Figure 23. Commercial Appeal, *October 31, 1920.*

S. TENN., THURSDAY MORNING, JUNE 23, 1921.—SIXTEEN PAGES.

THE SMOKE THAT TARNISHES.

Figure 24. Commercial Appeal, *June 23, 1921*.

TENN., TUESDAY MORNING, AUGUST 21, 1923.—TWENTY PAGES.

HIS "NOBLE WORK." DONE IN THE DARK!

Figure 25. Commercial Appeal, *August 21, 1923*.

JUNE 28, 1924.

A FREAK IN THE POLITICAL ZOO.

Figure 26. Commercial Appeal, *June 28, 1924*.

RNING, SEPTEMBER 10—TWENTY-EIGHT PAGES.

"WE WON MAINE FOR COOLIDGE!"
(Now Turn the Picture Upside Down.)

Figure 27. Commercial Appeal, *September 10, 1924*.

THE SMOKE THAT TARNISHES

Alley's depiction of mob justice (see Figure 24) is at once frightening and powerful. In this case, he was castigating the phenomenon of brute force and terrorism.

"NOBLE WORK," DONE IN THE DARK

Alley's comment on midnight floggings perpetuated by, but not directly associated with, the Ku Klux Klan is alarming and demonstrated the intolerance and social violence in American and regional history in the 1920s (see Figure 25).

A FREAK IN THE POLITICAL ZOO

Here Alley produced a phantasmagoric image of what can only be termed a nightmarish monster combining both major political parties into the Ku Klux Klan (see Figure 26). The meaning of the cartoon is nothing if not clear.

GOP MASK

By turning this cartoon on its head, this unique image further identified the Republican Party with the Klan (see Figure 27).

NO WONDER HE PUTS A SACK OVER THAT MUG!

Alley's cartoon is disturbing yet righteous as the hooded Klansman removes his mask only to reveal the hideous ogre that symbolized the freakish KKK member's bigoted personality (see Figure 28). Note that in the second frame the Klan member wears a straitjacket.

Left: Figure 28. *September 18, 1923.*

Below, left: Figure 29. Commercial Appeal, *March 24, 1917.*

Below, right: Figure 30. Commercial Appeal, *October 28, 1917.*

GOD GIVE US PEACE

As America entered into the First World War, Alley reflects the general American mindset that Germany was the cause for the conflict and that to resolve the issue the Kaiser's government and armies must be defeated (see Figure 29). His use of biblical symbolism is startling.

RIGHT OVER THE TOP!

Utilizing a combination of athletic prowess of trench warfare imagery, Alley celebrates the success of the Liberty Loan (see Figure 30). The flag-waving hurdler in the forefront appears to be Alley's self-portrait.

ARE YOU A SLACKER?

It was necessary for the federal government to borrow money in order to carry out America's commitment to the Allied cause. The term "Slacker" was a pejorative that was used as character assassination for those who neither bought "Liberty Bonds" nor supported the war in general. The single figure in the foreground is most likely Alley's caricature of himself (see Figure 31).

HIS FLAG AND YOURS

This cartoon image illustrated the impact of Liberty Loans, as the American "Sammy" (later to be called "Dough Boy") bravely charges into German trenches with the American flag attached to his bayonet (see Figure 32). German forces are symbolized by the craven Kaiser wearing a spiked helmet.

RSDAY MORNING, OCTOBER 25, 1917.—EIGHTEEN PAGES.

ARE **YOU** A SLACKER?

LIBERTY LOAN

ESDAY MORNING, OCTOBER 23, 1917.—SIXTEEN PAGES.

HIS FLAG—AND YOURS
OVER THE TOP WITH YOUR DOLLARS

Figure 31. Commercial Appeal, *October 25, 1917.*

Figure 32. Commercial Appeal, *October 23, 1917.*

AND OUR FLAG IS STILL THERE

National pride, martial patriotism, the flag, the Statue of Liberty and unending columns of allied soldiers are all combined here with the stalwart and determined image of a "Sammy" (see Figure 33). American war aims are easily identified. The medley of Alley's images could have been incorporated for the composite iconography seen in Frank Capra's "Why We Fight" in 1942.

THE TRIUMPH OF DEMOCRACY

The Teutonic blight of the earth—death—is embodied by a skull in a German spiked helmet, marking the Allied victory in 1918 (see Figure 34).

Figure 33. Commercial Appeal, *April 2, 1918.*

Figure 34. Commercial Appeal, *November 14, 1918.*

BETTER WAIT

The Teapot Dome scandal was prime material for the Democrat Alley. He was not averse to using cartoon balloons to depict the spoken word, although he seldom did so. Here "Miss Liberty" asks Uncle Sam if a special fund should be established to investigate corruption, to which he answers caustically that if he did investigate, it would probably be purloined (see Figure 35).

GOP CORRUPTION DISTILLERY

Alley's imaginative comment on the corruption then evident in the Republican Party illustrates the self-proclaimed yet tainted innocence associated with the Teapot Dome and other scandals (see Figure 36). His use of the visual imagery of politicians disobeying prohibition is unique and amusing.

HOT STUFF!

This cartoon symbolizes the then recent Teapot Dome scandal (see Figure 37). The over-boiling teapot takes a symbolic representation of the Republican Party's pain and embarrassment resulting from the affair's exposé.

BURGLARY INSURANCE

Alley shows a worried Uncle Sam running into the "Burglary Insurance" office after the 1924 general election victory of the GOP (see Figure 38). Uncle Sam hastens to protect the nation from such Republican scandals as the "Teapot Dome."

Figure 35. Commercial Appeal, *February 23, 1924.*

Figure 36. Commercial Appeal, *April 6, 1924.*

Figure 37. Commercial Appeal, *January 19, 1924.*

Figure 38. Commercial Appeal, *November 5, 1924.*

Figure 39. Commercial Appeal, *October 22, 1924.*

Figure 40. Commercial Appeal, *May 21, 1925.*

Figure 41. Commercial Appeal, *July 19, 1925.*

Figure 42. Commercial Appeal, *July 15, 1925.*

Oh Boy!

This political sketch was circulated by the Democratic National Committee in 1924 and won national attention for Alley's trenchant wit (see Figure 39). The lyrics are sung to the tune of a popular song of the time, "It Ain't Gonna Rain No More." The hesitant GOP elephant sings nervously as the stalwart Democratic Party sings with gusto. The use of mild profanity is not typical of Alley's work.

In Tennessee

While Alley demonstrated a progressive view in his work, he was also deeply religious. This sentiment was evident in his cartoon stimulated by the Tennessee legislature's passing of the Butler Act and subsequent "Monkey Trial" held in Dayton, Tennessee (see Figure 40). Evidently, he believed outside agitators were responsible for the trial.

Publicity

The ballyhoo of the Jazz Age and the Scopes Trial could hardly be better represented than in this cartoon (see Figure 41).

Darrow's Paradise

Alley's opinion about pro-evolution advocate Clarence Darrow seems at least to manifest religious fundamentalism and a reaction against science and modernization (see Figure 42). Here the attorney for the defense of John Scopes at the "Monkey Trial" is condemned as the antichrist.

STUDIES IN CHARACTER

Judging from Alley's effort in this cartoon, agnosticism was at least a sign of depravity while religious faith only uplifted and enlightened humanity (see Figure 43). Attorney for the prosecution William Jennings Bryan, a forthright, religious man, is contrasted with a disconsolate portrait of Clarence Darrow. Nothing less than a battle between good and evil raged in Dayton, Tennessee.

HILLS OF HOPE

Here Alley reinforces his positive projection of the morally upright Christian William Jennings Bryan, whose stand against the theory of evolution he considered truthful (see Figure 44).

Figure 43. Commercial Appeal, *July 23, 1925.*

Figure 44. Commercial Appeal, *July 28, 1925.*

FRIDAY MORNING, NOVEMBER 14, 1919.—TWENTY FOUR PAGES.

LET'S FINISH HIM ONCE FOR ALL!

Figure 45. Commercial Appeal, *November 14, 1919.*

SNUFFED OUT!

BOLSHEVIK TORCH-BEARER

Figure 46. Commercial Appeal, *February 19, 1919.*

FINISH HIM OFF ONCE AND FOR ALL

Alley's reaction against labor unions in general and the International Workers of the World (IWW) in particular is evident in this cartoon that implicated communists and leftist revolutionaries then persecuted in America during the postwar "Red Scare" (see Figure 45).

SNUFFED OUT!

Uncle Sam's star-studded hat eliminates revolutionary Bolshevik fervor, symbolized by a burning torch, and so saves America from destruction by American and foreign communists (see Figure 46).

ING, OCTOBER 14, 1924.—TWENTY-SIX PAGES.

SEEDS OF CORRUPTION.

Left: Figure 47. Commercial Appeal, *October 14, 1924.*

Below, left: Figure 48. Commercial Appeal, *March 24, 1921.*

Below, right: Figure 49. Commercial Appeal, *August 24, 1923.*

TENN., THURSDAY MORNING, MARCH 24, 1921.—TWENTY-TWO PAGES

A LITTLE THOUGHT FOR THOUGHTFUL PARENTS.

TENN., FRIDAY MORNING, AUGUST 24, 1923.—TWENTY-TWO PAGES.

THE TRIALS OF A CARTOONIST.

SEEDS OF CORRUPTION

Alley's concern for the weakening of the moral fortitude of American youth is evident in this cartoon (see Figure 47). A well-dressed teenage boy, smoking a cigarette, thumbs approvingly through magazines that display titillating and morally damaging narratives and illustrations.

A THOUGHT FOR THOUGHTFUL PARENTS

Hollywood movies posed dangers to young, impressionable minds, as Alley portrayed by placing two children at a movie marquee advertising salacious films (see Figure 48).

THE TRIALS OF A CARTOONIST

This multi-paneled presentation depicts the difficulties of editorial cartooning (see Figure 49). The artist shown was most likely another depiction of Alley himself. The newspaper artist had to be careful of what group he might offend, a caution familiar to many contemporary editorial cartoonists.

11

MYLES F. HORTON, TENNESSEE'S "RADICAL HILLBILLY"

THE HIGHLANDER FOLK SCHOOL AND EDUCATION FOR SOCIAL CHANGE IN AMERICA, THE SOUTH AND THE VOLUNTEER STATE

Born in Savannah, Tennessee, on July 9, 1905, one Tennessean would become a major protagonist in social justice movements in America. Through his leadership of the Highlander Folk School, Myles F. Horton would train and educate people to take action on their own initiative to better their lives by self-help and organized community action. Nothing in his family history suggested a predilection for social activism or controversial politics. His father, Joshua Horton, was among the original 1769 pioneers who were the first to settle at the Wataugua Settlement. His family usually voted Republican in the preponderantly Democratic South, and his father, Perry, a civil servant, was adamantly opposed to labor unions. The Hortons were members of the Cumberland Presbyterian Church.

His reverent parents believed firmly in the value of education as a means of getting ahead in life, and consequently Horton was a studious and religious boy who by 1924 had entered Cumberland University in Lebanon, Tennessee, where he pursued a major in literature. While he pursued the classics, young Horton spontaneously learned about social conflict, as demonstrated in his personal revolt against freshman hazing at university.

Social conflict was also apparent to Horton in the famous 1925 Scopes trial in Dayton, Tennessee, which fired his imagination. His membership in the Young Men's Christian Association (YMCA) unexpectedly introduced him to labor unions. In a speech to the YMCA in Lebanon during his tenure as president of the National Association of Manufacturers, John Emmett

Edgerton, a Chattanooga textile manufacturer, spoke negatively of labor unions and workers, saying that industrialists alone could claim the right to make social decisions for wage earners. Horton found this idea undemocratic and repugnant, sentiments that would hold for the rest of his life.

In the summer of 1927, Horton took a job instituting Presbyterian summer Bible schools in Cumberland County, then in the throes of economic collapse. In the small town of Ozone, according to historian Frank Adams in his *Unearthing Seeds of Fire: The Idea of Highlander*, Horton found the work "neither exciting nor challenging." He discovered that the songs, sermons and games of summer Bible school had little relation to the "daily problems faced either by the children or their hard-pressed parents." As Horton would say later: "I couldn't put this into words, but such education failed to connect with their lives." In Ozone, he found a way to make that connection; he decided to ask parents to come to the church at night to talk about their problems—and to his surprise, they did. If Horton couldn't answer the questions, he would find someone who could. He called these "community meetings," where neighbor met neighbor, and often they were able to provide answers to community problems. Then the mountaineers would try out what they had learned back home in the hollows. The distinction between "knowledge" and "practice" was becoming more precise to young Horton.

Upon graduating from Cumberland University in 1928, Myles took a summer job as the student YMCA secretary for Tennessee. His position allowed him to travel throughout the state, organizing illegal interracial YMCA meetings, a practice that earned him the enmity of white college and high school officials, who reported him to his YMCA superiors. His resignation was straightaway accepted, and soon Horton began study at Union Theological Seminary in New York City.

Soon after his arrival in New York, the stock market crashed, gigantic corporations went bankrupt and the city's unemployed were forming bread and soup lines. At school, Horton learned liberal theology best summarized by the teachings of Reinhold Neibuhr and the educational philosophy of John Dewey. He studied for a year with the famed Chicago sociologist Dr. Robert E. Park and learned about conflict and social movements. Through it all, Horton kept the "Ozone Project," as he came to call it, in mind, wondering if a new kind of school might be established to meet the singular needs of the mountain people in Tennessee. Finally, he managed to travel to Denmark in the summer and fall of 1931 and witnessed the working of the Danish folk schools. Here he found a workable model for his Ozone Project.

He returned home believing that he must embrace the everyday notions of the poor and educate them to act and speak for themselves and so gain influence over public decisions impacting their lives. These ideas would be central to the educational philosophy and operation of the folk school he was contemplating.

By November 1, 1932, Horton and colleagues had moved into a Grundy County location that would become known as the Highlander Folk School in Summerfield, between Monteagle and Tracy City. Soon, Horton found himself embroiled in the first of what would be a long series of immersions in the struggles for equity for the oppressed. In 1932, a particularly difficult strike occurred at the coal company town of Wilder-Davidson in Fentress County. He conducted food drives in Nashville to provide relief to striking miners—the Red Cross furnished supplies only to the strikebreakers. Horton was even arrested by national guardsmen and charged with "coming here and getting information and going back and teaching it." Ultimately, the strike at Wilder-Davidson was broken, but Horton realized that teaching could be a realistic force in bringing about social change in the South—but only if it were done within the experiential context of the common people, even if it included nonviolent resistance. As Horton wrote to one of his colleagues in early 1933:

> *The tie-in with the conflict situations and participation in community life keeps our school from being a detached colony or utopian venture...our efforts to live out our ideals makes possible the development of a bit of proletarian culture as an essential part of our program of workers' education.*

Highlander initially tutored neither reading, writing, working skills nor social acquiescence. It did, like its Danish example, teach basic skills and knowledge, yet nothing taught at Highlander sanctioned worker submission to exploitation. The educational philosophy at the Highlander Folk School demonstrated a commitment to instituting mutual aid among people and their subsequent organized confrontation of various interests for the public good. The Highlander would teach and empower, not lead.

For example, in 1936–39, Horton led community and union organizing drives, teaching previously unregistered voters about government. At one time, voters gained control of the Grundy County Commission and the WPA money it allocated. While initially successful, this led to a controversy ultimately won by state and county officials, a reversal that taught Horton two valuable lessons: trying to help powerless people win authority over a political unit as small as a county must certainly face defeat, and social change could not come from the ballot box but from education. Afterward, his energies were directed toward connecting education with expanding the growth of the unionization movement in the South.

His first involvement with labor unionization occurred with textile operatives in a North Carolina company town in 1937. Horton's work there consisted of helping in the formation of a union but more than that in teaching the workers how to control, run and use their union to gain their objectives. In a sense, he was helping to energize the previously dependent workers. Maintaining a commitment to local control, Horton firmly believed that the workers had to decide for themselves whether or not to strike. A union was formed, winning recognition and eventually a pay increase. Horton learned that dealing with one strike at a time did not constitute a social movement and that a strike generated working-class consciousness and enthusiasm for self-help. *The WPA Guide to Tennessee* (1939) described the Highlander as:

> *One of the few training schools for labor leaders in the South. In two small buildings, whose size helps to limit the student body to about 20, the school offers informal, discussion type lectures on cultural and economic subjects...*
>
> *A year-around community and county program is carried on and members of the school attempt to preserve the culture of the mountain people.*

Horton's educational efforts resulted in the formation of many workers' unions in the South. For instance, in 1938 an alumni had organized textile workers in Louisville, Kentucky, while in 1940 the Highlander helped in the formation of a union among aluminum workers at Alcoa, Tennessee, and in 1941 with the unionization of workers in New Orleans, Louisiana. By 1942, it was noted that some 90 percent of Highlander's graduates were international union officials, local union leaders or labor organizers in the South. Moreover, the Congress of Industrial Organizations (CIO), United Automobile Workers (UAW) regularly supported the school by sending members to participate in the regularly scheduled Highlander School's organizer training programs. It appeared that the union movement and the Highlander were almost permanently bound, but differences of opinion over union militancy and racial discrimination led to a parting of the ways. By 1952, Horton had come to believe that better race relations should be the school's new focus, especially since racism seemed to him to be the major stumbling block to the growth of unionism in the South.

The Highlander Folk School exhibited an early interest in the struggle for civil rights. Horton had shown interest in integration when he worked briefly for the YMCA. In 1935, the convening of the first (and last) All Southern Conference for Civil and Trade Union Rights (ASCCTUR) in Chattanooga was a Highlander project. The meeting of this biracial group was quickly broken up by uniformed crypto-fascist American Legionnaires, members of their post's "Americanization committee, some Chattanooga policemen and several local politicians." Conference participants were called Reds by the committeemen and forced to leave Chattanooga. The Conference retreated to Monteagle Mountain only after eluding their pursuers and sending them on a wild goose chase to Cleveland and Bradley County. At Highlander, resolutions were adopted against lynching and in favor of civil and union rights.

While the ASCCTUR dissolved, in November 1938, in Birmingham, Alabama, Horton joined in the first convening of the Southern Conference for Human Welfare (SCHW), also biracial. This organization, which existed until the late 1940s, advocated liberal reforms, including unionization, formation of sharecroppers' cooperatives and equal rights. Through such ties, blacks in increasing numbers began to attend illegal classes at the Highlander—illegal, that is, because they were integrated. Joining the school's board of directors were notable African American intellects and leaders such as Fisk University sociologist Dr. Lewis Jones and Dr. P.A. Stephens of Chattanooga. It became clear to Horton, however, that the struggle for equal rights hinged on ending racism in southern institutions. The 1950s would be a time of controversy, setbacks and turmoil for Highlander, an interval in which Horton ultimately would prevail.

As part of his civil rights educational initiative, Horton began night Citizenship Schools for African Americans starting with Johns Island

Portrait of Myles F. Horton. *Courtesy of the Nashville Room, Nashville Public Library.*

off shore from Charleston, South Carolina, in 1959. These schools were operated and taught by blacks and covered literacy while they provided basic information on voter registration and the electoral process to its students, who used the information to good effect in local elections. Horton believed strongly that these schools should be run by African Americans, who could better lead and identify with their own constituencies than whites.

Such Highlander-sanctioned Citizenship Schools were formed throughout the South. The classes also presented participants with practical knowledge about public policy formulation and its execution. Schools were attended by such civil rights leaders as Mrs. Rosa Parks and Nobel Peace Prize–winner Dr. Martin Luther King Jr. The existence of these schools led to bitterly active opposition by white supremacists in the 1950s. Such antagonism was usually justified by what historian Adams calls "the communist-racist masquerade." Indeed, one of the major controversies in the Highlander's history revolves around the specious belief that the school was "communistic."

Horton was not unused to hearing complaints of "communist influence" at the Highlander, a pejorative heard nearly from the beginning. Now, along with the history of teaching students how to organize labor unions and sharecroppers' associations, Horton was instructing biracial classes in methods of nonviolent resistance at Highlander. Scores learned skills and gained the fortitude to persist in their struggle for freedom, but some whites came to conflicting conclusions. A number of serious attacks were initiated from out of state during these waning years of the 1950s McCarthy era. The first attack was by an undercover agent for Georgia's white supremacist governor Marvin Griffin. The spy attended a special Labor Day weekend Citizenship School in 1957. He wrote a report with a paranoid claim that:

They met…and discussed methods and tactics of precipitating racial strife and disturbance.

The meeting of such a large group of specialists in inter-racial strife under the auspices of a Communist Training School, and in the company of many known Communists is the typical method whereby leadership training and tactics are furnished to the agitators.

According to Adams, Governor Griffin and Highlander's adversaries reprinted the report as a pamphlet employing the "technique of guilt by association." Photographs of Horton with Aubrey Williams, Dr. King and Mrs. Parks started appearing on southern billboards with huge letters proclaiming, "King Attended a Communist Training Center." The white

Teaching methods of passive civil disobedience and community organizing at the Highlander in the 1950s. Horton, Dr. Martin Luther King Jr. and an unidentified student are shown. *Courtesy of the Nashville Room, Nashville Public Library.*

supremacists soon found their campaign had backfired. Liberal patrons from throughout the nation publicly condemned Griffin. The effort to discredit the Highlander ultimately failed. Horton began to see a relationship between the increased antagonism expressed against Highlander and the growing civil rights movement. Horton had weathered this storm and had not compromised the Highlander or his principles.

Another attack initiated from out of state in 1959 would, however, force a compromise. Early that year, the attorney general of Arkansas, Bruce Bennett, made a speech warning the Tennessee legislature of subversion in the Volunteer State. He was quoted as saying, "I would gladly come to Tennessee if invited to lend whatever help I could to close Highlander." Bennett's remarks prompted the Tennessee legislature into action, and it immediately launched an investigation of the school. Accompanying state senator Lawrence T. Hughes and representatives Harry Lee Senter and T. Allen Hanover, Attorney General Bennett presided over the inquiry, which opened in Tracy City in February 1959. Aside from discovering the school was registered in Fentress and not Grundy County, nothing of any damaging nature was revealed, and the proceedings were moved to Nashville. In the capital city, the Arkansan tried to connect Highlander to various individuals or groups who had been accused of affiliation with various "communist front organizations," charging the school and its founder with complicity in a "communist conspiracy." On the stand, Horton was asked if he would acknowledge the accusations made about his politics. He refused, did not plead his Fifth Amendment rights and remained on the stand for four and a half hours. The hearings continued until March 6, 1959. According to an editorial in the March 7, 1959 *Nashville Tennessean*: "[The] two-act drama...had some interesting casting and some dialogue in which the so-called 'villains' outperformed the so-called 'heroes'...[However, it] was pretty much the dud of advance predictions."

Absolutely no evidence was found linking Highlander to subversive groups, and consequently, the committee could not make a finding revealing communist connections. Nevertheless, the attorney general of Tennessee, Albert Sloan, filed suit to revoke Highlander's charter. On July 31, at 8:30 p.m., Attorney General Sloan led a party of twenty sheriff's deputies and state troopers to Highlander in a search for alcoholic beverages. Since Grundy County was dry, possession or sale of alcohol was illegal. No whiskey was found anywhere on the school premises, but an empty whiskey barrel, as well as a trifling amount of gin, was discovered in Horton's personal quarters. His home was his private property and as such not covered by the warrant. Nevertheless, on the basis of such evidence, the entire biracial group attending the Highlander Citizenship School was arrested and summarily jailed. Horton, then serving as co-chair for an international conference on adult education in Europe, hurried home to Tennessee once he got word of the raid. Perhaps no better proof that allegations of subversion and communist affiliation made against the Highlander were inaccurate can be offered than the facts that the original warrant was thrown out of court and Attorney General Sloan's remark quoted in the August 3, 1959 *Chattanooga Daily Times* indicated there were no radical ties to the Highlander: "The members of the legislative committee gave me information mostly on integration and communism, and I wasn't satisfied I could be successful at that. I thought maybe this was the best shot and I think now I'll be successful."

Finally, Sloan got a temporary injunction, and Highlander's main building was padlocked. To keep the Citizenship Schools operating, Horton eventually was forced to transfer its function to the Southern Christian

Leadership Conference (SCLC) in 1961. While leading a workshop from makeshift quarters in October 1959, he confidently said, "You can padlock a building. You can't padlock an idea. Highlander is an idea. You can't kill it and you can't close it in. This workshop is part of the idea. It will grow wherever people take it."

In the meantime, the case of the *State of Tennessee v. Highlander* went to court. The trial ended in February 1960 with Judge Chester C. Chattin ruling that Highlander had sold beer and convenience items without a license, that the school was operated for Horton's personal gain and that it had practiced racial integration in violation of Title 49, Section 3701 of Tennessee law forbidding such practice.

The school's charter was revoked, and a receiver was appointed to liquidate the property. Expecting the worst, Horton had already applied for a new charter, which was granted. On August 28, 1961, the Highlander Research and Education Center, Inc., was opened in a dilapidated mansion in Knoxville near the Tennessee Marble Company plant. In December, the Summerfield property was sold at public auction. According to Adams, "No cent of compensation was ever paid to Horton or to his parents for the seizure of their private property. In an ironic footnote, lawyers from the Grundy area bought Highlander's library and turned the building into a private club." The original summer cottage caught fire and burned soon after the auction.

The concept of using education to foster social change was a basic tenet of Horton's learning philosophy. This Tennessean's principles helped produce the leaders to direct the activities of the civil rights movement of the 1960s. This basic idea resulted in the Montgomery Bus Boycott, a wave of peaceful sit-ins starting in Nashville in November and December 1959, school desegregation initiatives, the tempering of the Student Nonviolent Coordinating Committee (SNCC) in the civil rights struggle of the 1960s and, ultimately, the Civil Rights Act of 1964.

By 1964, Horton wanted to direct Highlander's didactic initiatives to Appalachia. He was particularly put off by the growth of welfare in the region after the collapse of the coal mining industry. He led workshops on self-education for small groups aimed at promulgating a "dialogue among nonequals" sponsored by the Tennessee Community Action Program (TCAP) directors in 1969 and held at Montgomery Bell State Park. His efforts resulted in local initiatives in the "war on poverty" program launched by President Lyndon B. Johnson.

After strengthening its commitment to Appalachia, Highlander moved from Knoxville to New Market, Tennessee, in 1972. Horton announced his resignation on May 28, 1973, but neither he nor the Highlander ceased labors to use education for the practical purpose of solving human problems, to teach ordinary people to meet their own challenges and create beneficial social change. According to his recent autobiography, *The Long Haul* (1990), "The best educational work at Highlander has always taken place when there is a social movement."

Myles F. Horton died of cancer at age eighty-four on January 19, 1990, at his home. In his last years, he spoke out against the "Moral Majority," saying, "They want to form a theocracy, and they want to be the 'theos.'" Private graveside services were held in Monteagle, near the site of the original school. An educator as well as a political and social activist, once describing himself as a "radical hillbilly," Horton dedicated his life's work to attaining an equitable social order ruled by human—not political or economic—relationships. Stressing equality and nonviolence instead of hate and political dogma, Myles F. Horton was a Tennessean in whom all of his fellow citizens can take pride. His life and work are more than a stitch in the rich tapestry of Tennessee's variegated history of contributions to the history of social change in the Volunteer State, the South and the nation.[17]

NOTES

1. For more information about William Walker, see Albert A. Carr, *The World and William Walker* (New York: Harper and Row, 1963); *Nashville Sentinel*, January 25, 1925; William O. Scroggs, *Filibusters and Financiers* (New York: MacMillan, 1916); Walter W. Crites, *American West* 9, no 6 (November 1972).

2. For more information, see Robert E. Corlew, *Tennessee: A Short History* (Knoxville: University of Tennessee Press, 1990); M.I. Phillips, *The Governors of Tennessee* (Gretna, LA: Pelican Publishing Company, 2002); J. Eugene Lewis, "The Tennessee Gubernatorial Campaign and Election of 1894," *Tennessee Historical Quarterly* 13, no. 3 (1954).

3. This subject was presented in greater detail in a paper delivered under the title "The Midland Railroad Subsidy Struggle of September 1887," at the April 2007 meeting of the Kentucky-Tennessee American Studies Association at Pleasant Hill Shaker Village, Kentucky.

4. William G. Thomas, *Lawyering for the Railroads: Business, Law, and Power in the New South* (Baton Rouge: Louisiana State Press, 1999), 108, 181–83, 185–86; James T. Moore, "Agrarianism and Populism in Tennessee, 1880–1915: An Interpretive Overview," *Tennessee Historical Quarterly* 42, no. 1 (1983): 76–94. The L&N records held at the Louisville University Archives do not reflect the 1887 controversy in Nashville.

5. Connie L. Lester, "John H. McDowell, 1844–post 1911," "Agricultural Wheel" and "Colored Agricultural Wheel," Tennessee Encyclopedia of History and Culture, http://tennesseeencyclopedia.net; James B. Jones Jr., "'General' John Hugh ('Jehazy') McDowell: A Brief Biography of

NOTES

a Confederate Veteran and Political Maverick (1844–1927)," *Courier*, October 1998.

6. James T. Moore, "Agrarianism and Populism in Tennessee, 1886–1896: An Interpretive Overview," *Tennessee Historical Quarterly* 42, no. 1 (1983): 80.

7. Joseph H. Cartwright, *The Triumph of Jim Crow: Tennessee Race Relations in the 1880s* (Knoxville: University of Tennessee Press, 1976). The example of robust black voter participation in this 1887 referendum seems contrary to Cartwright's well-established arguments.

8. Kincaid A. Herr, *The Louisville & Nashville Railroad: 1850–1940, 1941–1959* (Louisville, KY, 1959), 4–5, 8.

9. *Nashville Daily American*, August 11 and 18, 1887.

10. For example, see *Nashville Banner*, March 18, 1885.

11. *Nashville Daily American*, September 17, 1887; Robert H. Wiebe, *The Search for Order, 1877–1920*, American Century Series, edited by David Donald (New York, 1967), 1–2, 18–19, 23, 47–49, 52–53, 186.

12. *Commercial Appeal*, April 17, 1934 (obituary).

13. Alley was also the originator of the nationally syndicated comic strip *Hambone's Meditations*, which regardless of its humor is not included in this presentation. It is, however, the subject of an ongoing study. Alley's son, Calvin, continued with the *Hambone* series. The character was based on a black man Alley had known during his boyhood in Arkansas. Furthermore, *Hambone* was a composite of "many negro characters. His sayings were the creations of Mr. Alley's brain, of things he had overhead or had been told by friends." Alley would sketch *Hambone* all week, and by Friday he would have completed a new group for syndication. *Commercial Appeal*, April 17, 1934.

14. A rough estimate shows a total of 3,500. None of the original drawings are known to be extant.

15. *Commercial Appeal*, April 17, 1934.

16. Charles Crawford, ed., *Cat Alley* (Memphis, TN: Memphis State University Press, 1973).

17. For more information about the Highlander Folk School and Myles F. Horton, see Frank Adams, with Myles Horton, *Unearthing Seeds of Fire: The Idea of the Highlander* (Winston-Salem, NC: John F. Blair, 1975); John Glen, *Highlander, No Ordinary School* (Knoxville: University of Tennessee Press, 1988); and Myles F. Horton, with Judith Kohl and Herbert Kohl, *The Long Haul: An Autobiography* (New York: Teachers College Press, 1990).

INDEX

INDEX

INDEX

INDEX

Lord, Mrs. James S. Pierce, president of the Southern Woman's League for the Rejection of the Susan B. Anthony Amendment 90

Lost State of Franklin 11, 12, 13, 15, 16, 17, 18, 19, 20, 35
founded 1784 12
legislative body 12

Louisville and Nashville (L&N) Railroad 61, 62, 63, 64, 65, 67, 69, 70, 71, 72, 74, 75, 76, 77, 78, 79, 80, 84

Loyal League 51

Lyon, A.A. 87

M

major general of the United Confederate Veterans of Tennessee 53

manifest destiny 39, 40, 41, 42

Martin, Governor Alexander 12, 17

mass demonstrations 25, 28

Maxwell House Hotel 58

McCall, John E. 53

McCarthy era 126

McDowell, General Charles 19

McDowell, John Hugh "Jehazy" 47, 48, 49, 50, 51, 52, 53, 54
debasing his uniform 54

McKinley, President William 57, 59

McMinnville Southern Standard 89

media network 28

Medical College at the University of Pennsylvania 39

Memorandum of Concessions of Westerners 16

Memphis Commercial Appeal 57, 99, 100, 101

Memphis, Tennessee 44, 47, 53, 54, 57, 62, 86, 99, 101

Mexican-American War 40

Midland Railroad 61, 62, 63, 67, 69, 71, 75, 76, 78, 79, 80, 81, 82, 83

midnight floggings 107

Mimms, A.L. 56

Miro, Governor Esteban 16

Mississippi River 15, 16
safe navigation 16

Monroe Doctrine 40, 43

Monroe, James 21

Monteagle Mountain 125

Monteagle, Tennessee 89, 92, 123, 130

Montgomery Bell State Park 129

Mooney, C.P.J. 100

Moral Majority 130

Morgan, Charles 43

Mosquito Coast 40

Murfreesboro, Tennessee 21, 23, 57

Murphy, M.P. 86

N

Nashville American 50

Nashville and Chattanooga (N&C) Railroad 62

Nashville Banner 61, 63, 64, 86

Nashville, Chattanooga and St. Louis Railroad 61

Nashville Daily American 61, 64

Nashville, Tennessee 36, 39, 40, 45, 51, 52, 58, 59, 61, 65, 69, 71, 72, 74, 75, 81, 84, 87, 88, 89, 91, 95, 123, 128, 129

National Association for the Advancement of Colored People 90

National Association of Manufacturers 121

National Association Opposed to Woman Suffrage 88

National Republican Party 21, 23

negotiations 15, 16

Neibuhr, Reinhold 122

New Market, Tennessee 129

New Orleans 26, 27, 40, 44, 124

New Orleans Crescent 40

New South 50, 99

Nicaragua 39, 40, 42, 43, 44, 45, 100

Nicholson, Alfred Osborne Pope 29
Nineteenth Amendment 85, 89, 92,
    101, 103, 104

North Carolina 11, 12, 13, 15, 16, 17,
    18, 19, 20, 31, 33, 34, 35, 124
  act of cession 11
Nye investigation (1935) 96

O

Obion County 32, 49, 53
Old Hickory 23, 25, 26, 27, 28
Old Pete 57
Old Tassel 15
Ozone Project 122
Ozone, Tennessee 122

P

pardons 17
Parker, Alton B. 53
Park, Robert E. 122
Parks, Rosa 126
Paste Pot affair 59
Patterson, Malcom R. 53
Pearson, Josephine A. 89, 90, 91, 92
People's Party 49, 50, 52
personal charisma 28
Pillow, Ernest 58
Pinkerton detectives 62, 64
plebiscite 12
political clothing 28
poll tax 56, 58, 59, 96
Populist Party 56, 62
Presbyterian summer Bible schools 122
prisoner-lease system 55
professional political organization 28
Progress and Poverty (1879 Henry George
    novel) 94
Progressive (or "Bull Moose") Party
    53, 54
Prohibition Party 49, 50, 56, 93
propaganda 25, 26, 89, 96
public subscription 62, 63

R

Raousset-Gabson, Count Gaston
    Raoul de 41
"real dirt farmers" 95
Reconstruction 49, 51, 57
Red Rose Brigade 91
Reds 125
referendum 62, 63, 64
Republican Party 21, 23, 49, 52, 55,
    56, 57, 58, 95, 100, 101, 104,
    107, 112
Roberts, Governor Albert H. 91, 92
Roche, Samuel S. 76, 78
Rogersville, Tennessee 88
Roosevelt, Theodore 54, 59, 95
Rush, Richard 23

S

San Francisco 40, 41
San Francisco Commercial-Democrat 42
San Francisco Herald 41
San Jacinto, Nicaragua 45
San Jose, Costa Rica 45
San Juan River 41, 44
Savannah, Tennessee 121
Scopes trial 101, 115, 121
secession 11, 15, 20
  East Tennessee from the Volunteer
    State 32
Senter, Harry Lee 127
Sevier, John 13, 15, 16, 17, 18, 19, 20
  arrested on charges of treason 19
  oath of allegiance to North
    Carolina 20
  relinquished the field 18
  sons 19
Shelby County 54
Shelby, Evan 19
Sloan, Albert 128
social change 121, 123, 124, 129, 130
Socialist Party 93, 94, 96, 98
social movements 122, 124, 130
Sonora (Mexican province) 41, 42

INDEX

INDEX

W

Walker, William 39, 40, 41, 42, 43,
      44, 45
  executed (September 12, 1860) 45
war on poverty 129
Washington County 12, 18, 19
Washington, D.C. 32, 58, 98
Watauga Association (1772) 11, 12
Weakley County 32, 33
Weaver, Dr. Rufus W. 87
Weaver, General James B. 53, 87
Weekly Toiler 49, 50, 51, 52
Wheel and Alliance 50
Whig Party 28, 29, 30, 32
whisky rings 49
White, Congressman James 15
Wilder-Davidson, Tennessee 123
Wilson, Woodrow 54
Winstead, George W. 52
wool hat boys 50
WPA Guide to Tennessee (1939) 124

Y

Young Men's Christian Association
      (YMCA) 121, 122, 125

ABOUT THE AUTHOR

James B. Jones Jr. is the public historian on the staff of the Tennessee Historical Commission/State Historic Preservation Office in Nashville, Tennessee. He is the author of many articles dealing with Tennessee's nineteenth- and twentieth-century past and many books, including *The Hidden History of Civil War Tennessee* (The History Press, 2013). He studied at the University of Mississippi, earning a BA and MA in history, and at Middle Tennessee State University, where he took a DA in historic preservation and history. He lives with his wife, Cynthia, in Murfreesboro, Tennessee.

www.ingramcontent.com/pod-product-compliance
Lightning Source LLC
Chambersburg PA
CBHW060806100426
42813CB00004B/970